High Performance As A Goal

Achieving Excellence in Facility Management

James P. Whittaker, P.E., CFM, CEFP, FRICS
&
Teena G. Shouse, CFM, IFMA Fellow

www.feapc.com

Vision Spots Publishing
www.VisionSpotsPublishing.com

Copyright Notice

James P. Whittaker, President and CEO
Teena G. Shouse, VP of Corporate Services
Facility Engineering Associates, P.C. (FEA)
12701 Fair Lakes Circle, Suite 101
Fairfax, VA 22033
www.feapc.com

First Printing, 2013

ISBN-13: 978-1484992708

ISBN-10: 1484992709

Printed in the United States of America

Contents

Preface

The content of this book has been a long-time in the making. It was conceived by professionals who questioned the norm and truly wanted to change the way Facility Managers evaluate the health of their organizations and *make them better*. The goal was to develop an approach that asks the right hard questions which would lead them to answers to help others achieve true operational excellence in Facility Management (FM). Most importantly, our approach to Facility Management organization evaluation and improvement has been developed over the past three decades by drawing on our experiences from working with hundreds of true professionals in the FM industry across the U.S. and abroad.

The approach to resolve challenges through relevant solutions shared in this book have been drawn from some of the best Facility Managers within government agencies, colleges and universities, public school systems, healthcare organizations, cultural facilities, research institutions and corporate facility organizations. Additionally, we have incorporated our own Facility Engineering Associates (FEA) team experience gained through consulting engagements, operating and maintaining facilities, as well as years of researching and teaching Facility Management competencies. This book explores many best practices in Facility Management and provides an assessment approach to evaluate the capabilities and the process maturity level of a FM organization.

The culmination of our experience and research has resulted in an assessment and improvement approach we named fmDiagnostics™. fmDiagnostics™ incorporates standardized Facility Management organization best practices processes and procedures, a capability maturity model, lean process evaluation methodologies, and industry standards. It is a comprehensive organizational, leadership, and process diagnostic approach developed specifically to measure FM performance and help create high performance (world class) facilities organizations. fmDiagnostics™ utilizes this systematic process to evaluate the performance of your Facility Management organization from the organizational, process and technology perspectives. It goes well beyond basic benchmarking. By incorporating decades of expertise and experience from seasoned FM professionals and recognized industry best practices, benchmarks and standards, we created a solution that incorporates *realistic, practical and proven* recommendations to improve effectiveness and efficiencies.

The fmDiagnostics™ approach is organized in a Baldrige framework of performance categories that incorporate capability maturity model concepts and links to FM Key Performance Indicators (KPIs). We chose to utilize the Capability Maturity Model (CMM) as the yardstick for measuring the current and desired level of effectiveness based on the answers given on a comprehensive assessment questionnaire. Additionally, recommendations to improve organizational capabilities and reach the next level of performance are presented based on the level of organizational maturity within each performance category. Some of the concepts from recognized resources used to develop fmDiagnostics™ methodology include:

- Top management models and concepts researched and summarized by the American Management Association (AMA).
- Balanced Scorecard Performance Measurement Methodology (BSPMM) published by the Harvard Business School.
- Baldrige National Quality Program (BNQP) quality measurement system.

- International Facility Management Association (IFMA) global job task analyses, core competencies and performance areas, as well as Facility Management benchmark reports.
- Association of Higher Education Facilities Officers (APPA) Body of Knowledge (BOK) areas and performances.
- National Research Council/Federal Facilities Council (NRC/FFC) framework for effective facility asset management, including governing mind-sets, behaviors, and approaches, as well as organizational capabilities, individual skills, and essential areas of expertise.

We have utilized the fmDiagnostics™ approach to successfully evaluate and improve the performance of many facility organizations managing K-12 schools, colleges and universities, healthcare, corporate headquarters, and local and federal government facilities. We cultivate the opportunity for enhanced performance to be measured and linked to long-term performance measures which will validate the value of the Facility Management organization. fmDiagnostics™ has also been instrumental in helping to create high performance FM organizations that fully support strategic business initiatives, enhance operational efficiencies and effectiveness, and reduce short-term operating and long-term capital replacement costs.

The fmDiagnostics™ approach has also proven to be valuable as an educational tool to introduce students and transitioning professionals to the breadth of requirements and best practices of Facility Management organizations. Specific examples of lean process improvements, FM technology enhancements, and alignment of strategic FM planning with operations and maintenance practices have been incorporated from some of the most experienced FM professionals across the U.S.

To complement our literary efforts in this book and tie the industry needs to our solution, we have solicited advice from some of the most experienced and recognized Facility Management experts in the field. An entire chapter is devoted to sharing their stories and advice on relevant issues related to current FM topics, trends, and the future of the profession.

Bottom-line – this book was written to enable FM organizations to identify needed changes, continuously monitor improved performance excellence, build pride in their organization, and better attract and retain much needed quality employees. The outcome of following the fmDiagnostics™ method of assessment is a strategic plan including practical recommendations designed to help optimize the performance of your Facility Management organization. It has been designed to take an owners perspective of facilities and help Facility Managers tell the story of how they have, or will, create a high performance organization which best supports the mission of the parent organization.

This self-assessment process is for those FM professionals who are willing to work hard, be honest with themselves and others about where their organization currently is, and visualize how great it can be in the future. If you are one of those brave individuals, enjoy the journey of self-awareness and opportunities to create a truly world class FM organization.

Foreword

W hy should Facility Managers have the capabilities to create a High performance Facility Management Organization? I think the answer is quite simple. It is impractical to suggest that a Facility Manager could provide the desired level of high performance facilities that so many of today's business leaders seek without the capacity to organize and deliver the skills, experience, and knowledge required for the development of such an organization.

I relish opportunities to exchange thoughts with other FM professionals on particularly interesting subjects, especially when they are relevant to how our profession is perceived as a critical enabler of business success. So I typically like to begin these discussions by establishing a mutual frame of reference, usually with an acceptable definition from an authoritative source, so our dialogue can at least share a common perspective. In its report to Congress, the High performance Building Council (part of the National Institute of Building Sciences) stated, "High performance buildings, which address human, environmental, economic and total societal impact, are the result of the application of the highest level design, construction, operation and maintenance principles — a paradigm change for the built environment."

It's commonly shared at national and international-level FM events that the global market landscape continues to force business leaders in the public, private and academic sectors, particularly those responsible for large and /or geographically separated real property portfolios, to seek answers on how to best manage their facilities and infrastructure to achieve greater efficiency and effectiveness. So more than ever, key questions frequently asked of Facility Managers by their leadership include, "Is the facility portfolio strategically aligned to the future organizational goals?"; "What competencies should my workforce possess to address current trends & future outlook?"; and "How well should each of my facilities perform with respect to industry standards and expectations?"

In an era where continuing budget cuts, modernization, technological advances, and environmental sustainability continue to directly influence a shift in how we manage facilities, a "high performance" capabilities edge is needed by FMers to further validate how the services that our teams provide are vital to organizational business continuity and longevity. The Center for Creative Leadership published a 1999 report entitled, "High performance Work Organization: Definitions, Practices, and An Annotated Bibliography'" which stated that there was no generally accepted definition for high performance work organizations, or HIPOs. The Center's report did offer five components or dimensions of HIPO, as derived from the synthesized summary from leading scholars and researchers in this field of study: (1) self-managing work teams; (2) employee involvement, participation, empowerment; (3) total quality management; (4) integrated production technologies; and (5) the learning organization. A 2013-released eHow money article shared a definition that's very applicable in the context of the current trends and future outlook for the FM profession. According to the contributing author, "A high performance organization is a company that is considered more successful than its competitors in areas such as profitability, customer service and strategy".

2

So, as an FM practitioner with almost 30 years of combined service to the public, private and not-for-profit business sectors, much of that time working in a HIPO, I absolutely concur and endorse Jim Whittaker and Teena Shouse's definition of a high performance organization, and its applicability to one providing FM services. Armed with a standardized, systematic approach described by Jim and Teena to quantitatively measure data-based mission performance, as well as management's performance, these high performance FM organizations are uniquely suited to address the technological, environmental, geopolitical, and socio-economic trends affecting public and private sector facilities, as captured in current FM as well as Real Estate reports published in the US and Europe. An FM organization's ability to examine its organizational leadership effectiveness, strategic and operational planning capability, appropriate levels of customer focus, performance-based data and knowledge management, and results-driven workforce development, can help determine people, place, process and technological improvements needed to provide enhanced facility services, improved efficiency, and reduced O&M operating costs, in accordance with business strategic goals, and the desires of leaders who established them.

Congratulations to Jim and Teena on releasing their new book to help FM professionals across the globe create an FM HIPO that can better enable our ability to advance the performance of an organization's two most important assets – the workforce and the workplace.

Thomas "Tom" L. Mitchell, Jr., Lt Col (ret), USAF, CFM, CFMJ

Managing Director, Facilities and Asset Management Consulting Services, Booz | Allen | Hamilton

Chairman, 2009-2010 Board of Directors, International Facility Management Association

Director, Board of Directors, U.S. National Institute of Building Science

Chairman, Facility Management Academic Advisory Council, Florida A&M University

Introduction

Today's institutions, agencies, and businesses face unprecedented fiscal and social challenges. Leaders must deal with continued budget reductions, changing regulations, increased social and sustainability drivers, workplace threats, more complex and rapidly changing technologies, and the need for better data-driven decisions. These issues need to be carefully managed to maintain a high performance organization.

High performance Facility Management requires a careful balance of inputs such as energy, labor, materials and capital (both political and financial). Work processes such as; how we maximize space, utilize technology, and lead and manage our Facility Management workforce are those processes at which we need to excel. The desired output is a safe, healthy, comfortable and productive work environment while saving energy and operating in a cost effective manner. As we improve building systems to deliver high performance we will need to maintain a high performance environment in the delivery of Facility Management services.

This task is even more difficult considering the basic functions of Operations and Maintenance (O&M) have become more challenging due to the increasing complexity and automation of building systems. Simply managing the overwhelming amounts of facilities data to enable effective decision making is at a tipping point. It is no wonder that still today most Facility Management organizations are reactive in nature. Continuous improvement processes applied to FM organizations have typically garnered less than stunning results.

What is needed is a new perspective to produce real changes in creating high performance FM organizations. We must start with re-defining *"world class"* and *"high performance"* with respect to the FM organization. Then, practically and effectively implement structural and process changes to achieve the desired outcome. Finally, we must measure performance with meaningful KPIs and close the performance gap.

This is not simply a venture for new or changing FM organizations. Even mature Facility Management organizations can benefit from a regular review of organizational structure and characteristics, process reviews for efficiency, assessment of current conditions and forecast of future needs, and a continual review and improvement of the knowledge, skills, and abilities of Facility Management personnel. Like any organization, the Facility Management function should have high performance of the organization as a strategic objective. There should also be performance measures and metrics for determining if the Facility Management function is meeting that objective.

Although the structure of the Facility Management organization varies from industry to industry, the creation of a highly competent Facility Management department will help assure that the organizational strategy is aligned and followed. One way to ensure alignment and performance is to adopt a leadership philosophy of high performance both in the organization and the performance of the facility.

With the challenges presented to FM organizations come great opportunities. We believe that we are now at a tipping point in the FM profession. The spectrum of global economic challenges, changing codes and regulations, focus on environmental sustainability and energy conservation, increasingly complex building systems, vastly improved Facility Management technologies and standards have spurned the need for greater FM education. Universities and associations have responded with the development of more and more Facility Management degree programs, certification programs and FM credentials. Finally, the creation of an International Organization for Standardization (ISO) technical committee to develop guidance standards for the FM profession is helping to elevate the profession.

Facility Managers and Facility Management organizations make a positive contribution to the world in which we live. It's no longer just about providing safe, secure, and productive facilities. We must continually strive to improve our standards, promote best practices in the profession, and enable the mission of every organization for which we serve. This book has been prepared with these concepts in mind.

Chapter 1: High Performance as the Goal

A s we begin the journey to creating high performance facilities we must first define the goal. This is not as easy as one might first expect. There are multiple visions of what it might look like from the summit and multiple paths, or approaches to get there. This chapter begins to define high performance organizations and discusses best-in-class management models and organizational evaluation approaches. First, let's begin by defining Facility Management. The International Facility Management Association (IFMA) defines Facility Management as *"a profession that encompasses multiple disciplines to ensure functionality of the built environment by integrating people, place, processes, and technology"*.[1]

Defining High Performance Organizations

High performance organizations are those that are skilled at developing a strategy, implementing a plan to follow that strategy, operating with an effective performance management system, and constantly reassessing and adjusting their plan to meet an operating

---

[1] IFMA, FMPedia, http://ifmacommunity.org/fmpedia

and regulatory changing environment. Some of the key attributes of a high performance organization are that organizations include a:

- Strategic approach to the future of the organization
- High level strategy and planning skills
- An in-depth knowledge of their stakeholders
- Sound processes for accomplishing work
- Processes for continual improvement
- Commitment to the development of the workforce

High performance companies and organizations are models of the corporate world. They represent companies, agencies, and institutions that consistently outperform their peers and/or competitors. As we strive to improve our own organizations, we want to know more about what makes some organizations perform at the top of the spectrum.

There are also scores of facilities mission statements that speak of "*Providing world class services…*" or "*to create high performance facilities*", yet we have little ability to define world class or more importantly measure it. Some say it is the ability to consistently outperform all others in achieving a common mission. This leads to the importance of aligning the facilities services with the mission of the parent organization and developing sound metrics to prove the FM organization is performing well in its role of enabling the mission. A high performance Facility Management organization:

- Fully supports strategic business initiatives
- Enhances operational efficiencies/effectiveness
- Optimizes process performance
- Minimizes Total Cost of Ownership (TCO)
- Maximizes asset value and life cycle
- Continuously monitors improved performance

- Builds pride and attracts new employees

High performance Facility Management requires the knowledge, skills and abilities to deliver services at a high level, and the physical infrastructure to deliver those services in an economical, environmentally friendly, and people friendly workplace. The Facility Manager must carefully balance inputs such as energy, labor, materials and capital (both political and financial), to deliver quality services to the organization.

The Facility Manager does this by developing and implementing processes such as; real estate portfolio planning, work management, space management, continually monitoring customer feedback, and managing operating and capital budgets. Competencies and tools for the Facility Manager include; strategy and planning skills; a focus on the customer; dedication to improving the knowledge, skills, and abilities of the workforce; effective management of space and work; and the ability to measure, monitor and report progress toward economic and environmental goals.

The output of a successful and sustainable Facility Management program is a safe, healthy, comfortable and productive work environment while saving energy and resources, and operating in a cost effective manner. As we improve building systems to deliver high performance, we will need to maintain a high performance environment in the delivery of Facility Management services.

Management Models and Evaluation Approaches

There have been many leadership books, and countless business journal articles published on the topic of how to excel as an organization. Due to the complex and unique nature of organizations, these publications often raise as many questions as they provide answers. Despite these difficulties, researchers continue to attempt to identify and define the elements of a high performance organization. A summary of some relevant management models, theories and evaluation approaches is provided in the following sections.

AMA – One of the most thorough studies was commissioned by the American Management Association (AMA) and conducted by the Institute for Corporate Productivity. The High Performance Organization Survey 2007 compiled a substantial amount of research and survey data to help define what makes an organization *"high performance"*.

A review of the research indicated five key factors drive and influence organizational performance. Each element influences and interacts with the others as shown in Figure 1.

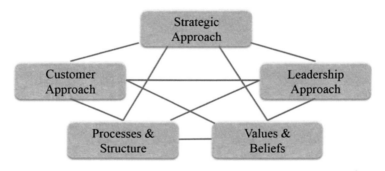

AMA Global Study
A Model of High-Performance Organizations

From Overholdt, Granell, Jargon. 2006. (AMA. 2007)

Figure 1: Interactive elements of a high performance organization

The research also reported that to create a high performance organization requires committing to adhering to the following principles:

1. Develop strategies that are consistent, clear, and well thought out.
2. Develop a superior service attitude that goes above and beyond for our clients.
3. Adhere to high ethical standards throughout the organization.
4. Provide leadership that is clear, fair, and talent-oriented.
5. Provide clear performance measures, training employees to do their jobs, and enabling employees to work together.
6. Promote the organization as a good place to work.
7. Allow employees to use their skills, knowledge, and experience to create unique solutions for our clients.

NRC – In 2008, the National Research Council (NRC) published the results of a study for the Federal Facilities Council (FFC) regarding core competencies in federal facilities asset management. The number one recommendation of the study stated, *"To effectively manage federal facilities portfolios through 2020 and beyond, federal organizations and their facilities asset management divisions should operate within the overall framework depicted below:"*

Framework for Effective Facilities Asset Management

Core Competencies for Federal Facilities Asset Management Through 2020: Transformational Strategies (NRC 2008)

Figure 2: Recommended framework for effective federal facilities asset management

The recommended framework advises federal facilities organizations to:

- Adopt the mind-set of an owner of facilities
- Adopt behaviors that integrate facilities-related decisions into strategic planning processes to support the organization's overall missions
- Use a life-cycle management approach to operate efficiently, reliably, and cost-effectively
- Measure performance to support continuous improvement of facilities asset management processes

To fully implement this approach it will require a new way of thinking about the organizational capabilities. The core competencies of the organization will require three essential areas of expertise and a broad skills base. The areas of expertise are *integrating* people, processes, places, and technology by using a life-cycle approach; *aligning* the facilities portfolio with the organization's mission and available resources; and *innovating* across traditional functional lines and processes to address changing requirements and opportunities. Implementing this framework is essential to generating performance excellence.

Baldrige – Performance excellence is a term used to describe high performance organizations. One of the leading international organizations that defined the criteria for performance excellence is The Foundation for the Malcolm Baldrige National Quality Award. In a public-private partnership with the National Institute of Standards and Technology (NIST) and others, the Foundation has developed the criteria for performance excellence as follows:

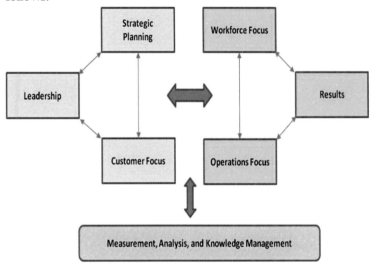

Figure 3: Baldrige Framework

This framework provides the guidance to those organizations that want to improve their results. Results are improved through strengthening the leadership triad (left side of the figure), and the results triad (right side of the figure). Performance and competitiveness is improved by linking these two triads through performance measurement and analysis, and effective knowledge management (at the bottom of the figure).

CMM – Another approach to organizational improvement is the Capability Maturity Model (CMM) developed at Carnegie Mellon University for the U.S. Department of Defense. The term *"maturity"* relates to the degree of formality and optimization of processes, from ad hoc practices, to formally defined steps, to managed result metrics, to active optimization of the processes (refer to Figure 4). An enhanced Capability Maturity Model Integration (CMMI) process improvement approach furthers the goal to help organizations improve their performance. CMMI can be used to guide process improvement across a project, a division, or an entire organization.

According to the Software Engineering Institute (SEI) 2008, CMMI helps *"integrate traditionally separate organizational functions, set process improvement goals and priorities, provide guidance for quality processes, and provide a point of reference for appraising current processes"*.

Characteristics of Organization Maturity Levels

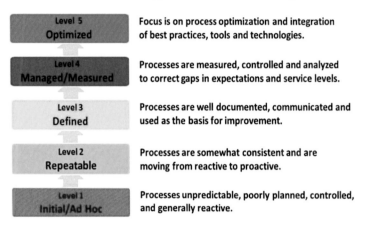

Figure 4: Capability Maturity Model levels

BEM2/3 – Researchers at the University of Applied Sciences FH Kufstein Tirol in Austria presented a process capability assessment tool to identify process maturity levels in the *"built environment"* in various industries. The tool is called *"Built Environment Management Model (BEM2/BEM3)"*. The tool consists of a survey of 58 questions followed by a semi-structured interview process. The information is recorded in a database, which then calculates relative maturity scores based on the interview feedback.

The CMM levels are utilized wherein a high capability maturity score indicates that an organization has well defined, measured, managed and self-improving processes. While a low score indicates processes are conducted in an ad hoc fashion. The questions are grouped into four categories: strategic planning, built environment portfolio management, project management, and services/operations and maintenance management.

EFQM – EFQM is another process survey tool for Facility Management developed by EFQM and Philips Electronics. EFQM is a not-for-profit consortium of 14 leading European businesses. The survey tool considers four groups of key FM processes and three groups of FM key enablers that include a total of 19 FM elements covering the processes that take place within an FM organization. The groups of elements include:

FM Key Processes
• Customer relationship management
• Service portfolio management
• Service delivery management
• FM financial management
FM Key Enablers
• Strategic management
• Management support
• FM human resource management

A scale defining 11 maturity levels, starting at 0 and ending at 10 were developed to describe the maturity of the FM organization. Each of the 19 elements is then evaluated based on components within each maturity level.

FMEP – APPA's Facilities Management Evaluation Program (FMEP) provides higher-education institutions with a customized evaluation conducted by a team of institutional peers and based on a comprehensive set of criteria. Institutions receive a written report consisting of feedback and recommended actions which are personalized to each institution and designed to help transform participating educational facilities programs into those worthy of international recognition.

The FMEP Program is conducted in four stages. First, the institution's facilities team undertakes a *self-evaluation*, using criteria established by APPA[2]. Afterwards, an *onsite evaluation team* is organized by APPA, which meets with the facilities organization at the institution. While onsite, the evaluation team summarizes its findings in an *oral report*, which it provides to the facilities organization to substantiate its findings and gain clarification. Finally, after the onsite evaluation and oral report, the evaluation team produces a final *written report*, which is then delivered to the institution. Care is taken to ensure that the evaluation team is comprised of a select group of peers from campuses with similar educational, financial, and physical characteristics.

MMA – The Maintenance Management Audit (MMA) process was created in 1991 to provide a framework for organizations to systematically review, analyze, and recommend improvements in performance. The audit system was designed to identify the tasks of a facilities organization seeking to improve its effectiveness and efficiency. The process defines a step-by-step method of conducting a large scale audit of a facilities maintenance organization and provides direction in identifying areas that merit the most intensive investigation. It defines the basic components of the maintenance management audit as: 1) Organization, 2) Workload Identification, 3) Work Planning, 4) Work Accomplishment, and 5) Appraisal.

The MMA is narrowly focused on O&M productivity and efficiency of the FM organization. However, this early work was instrumental in helping to define opportunities to improve the effectiveness and efficiency of facilities work forces.

---

[2] APPA was originally founded as the American Physical Plant Association and later changed to the Association of Higher Education Facilities Officers. Today APPA is simply branded as "APPA – Leadership in Education".

Integrating FM and Performance

Building a high performance organization that achieves both Facility Management and organizational performance goals and objectives requires an approach that integrates the optimum components of these aforementioned bodies of work with practical experience. The authors through their efforts at FEA embraced this challenge and developed a systematic and comprehensive approach with a corresponding tool set that brings these components together.

In the following chapters, we will provide a context for the development of this approach, explain its components, how it is applied, and offer some case studies that illustrate it value and benefits.

Chapter 2: Development of High performance FM Organizations

For over two decades Facility Engineering Associates (FEA) has been venturing into facilities to not only evaluate the condition and performance of buildings and building systems, but to assess the performance of the organizations which operate and maintain them. Facility Managers and their organizations have come a long way in optimizing performance of facilities. However, it has become more challenging year after year. Building technologies have become more sophisticated. Building systems are more complex. Facility information is more abundant than ever. The regulatory environment is increasing and becoming stricter, impacting organizational operating structures and missions. There is an increased focus on sustainability and energy conservation. Reporting requirements have multiplied. All of these challenges have come with higher visibility, accountability and sometimes shrinking FM staffs and operating budgets.

The public has been demanding better operated schools, cleaner hospitals, more efficient transportation facilities, and fiduciary responsibility of taxpayer dollars in the stewardship of federal facilities. The focus has been on the Facility Manager to reduce operating costs, increase efficiency and effectiveness and optimize performance. While this has led to better education and training of Facility Managers, there has also been a greater need to better evaluate and measure performance.

FEA's professionals have worked in hundreds of facilities organizations to assess and optimize their performance over the years. The FM organizational evaluations have ranged from public school systems to colleges/universities, healthcare organizations and cancer research centers, local-state-federal government agencies, and corporate facilities. Each has had their own assessment protocol or requested consideration of their unique market elements. As an example, the State of Texas Legislative Budget Board has a standard protocol for independent school district performance evaluations that includes processes for facilities construction, use, and management. Similarly, other states such as Virginia, Maryland, Colorado, Massachusetts, and Wyoming have similar but unique school performance review standards. Universities often request FMEP evaluations through APPA to evaluate FM performance and generate recommendations for process improvements. Finally, government agencies have requirements to evaluate and report operational performance as part of government-wide performance improvement initiatives. However, the evaluations and reporting have not been standardized.

Our experience indicates that there are as many reasons for conducting the evaluations as there are projects. In many cases we have been asked by financial officers or business executives to *'audit'* FM organizations to provide an independent opinion of performance and opportunities to reduce or avoid costs. In a few cases we have been asked to help self-evaluate an organization prior to a larger internal or external audit. There have also been cases of known leadership transitions that have initiated reviews to generate a baseline and aid in succession planning. Lastly, some forward thinking organizations have requested evaluations simply to help improve performance.

All of these varying factors have led to inconsistent processes in evaluating organizations. Every evaluation required a new set of procedures and each report had to be laboriously re-written from scratch. These factors added to the substantial costs to every project.

Through this experience, we recognized the opportunity to standardize evaluation methods to increase consistency/accuracy, and provide better value to clients. We set out by researching standards incorporated into various approaches. The results at the time indicated *"there weren't any reliable standards".* This led to our decision to create the fmDiagnostics™ approach to evaluating and improving performance.

Planning the Expedition

You must possess individual skills and organizational capabilities. A strong Facility Manager will integrate across boundaries, align processes with the mission, and create a systematic and planned approach to the summit. They will assess the best route to the top, plan and visualize the summit, select the route, prepare the team, gather the tools, and implement the plan. Our suggested route for a successful expedition to the top is revealed in the following chapters.

fmDiagnostics™ is a standardized and systematic Facility Management organization and process evaluation and improvement system. We consider it the first true comprehensive organizational and leadership diagnostic tool developed specifically to measure FM performance and help create high performance facilities organizations. The overarching framework is based on the six performance categories established by the Baldrige Quality Program

23

for organizations. The categories include: Leadership, planning, customer service, workforce development, measurement, and processes.

The systems approach to FM evaluations incorporated into fmDiagnostics™ is based on best practices, benchmarks, and standards published by IFMA, APPA, and the NRC/FFC. fmDiagnostics™ approach also employs leadership assessment processes developed at the Harvard Business School (e.g., the balanced scorecard) and the Baldrige National Quality Program (BNQP) quality measurement system.

Current efforts include the incorporation of organizational capability maturity models developed at Carnegie Mellon University to enhance the organization and value of fmDiagnostics™ output.

Visualizing the Summit

So, what does a high performance (world class) FM organization look like? The following sections will take a look at what we consider level 5 facilities performance. It is a view from the summit. While there is not a one-size fits all answer, the common characteristics of a high performance organization most likely include the following:

Leadership: The FM organization is well structured and organized with clear lines of communication and responsibility. The leadership takes and owner's perspective and a strategic approach to decision making. FM leaders adhere to high ethical standards and encourage the same throughout the organization. They exhibit leadership characteristics that are clear, fair, and talent-oriented.

The FM strategy is visibly apparent, well publicized, regularly updated and obvious to everyone. The Mission, Vision, and Values (MVV) are aligned with the parent (demand) organization and understood by everyone in the FM organization. The leadership proactively solicits needs and expectations from customers across the parent organization and outside. The leadership also communicates short-term and long-term needs to executives clearly and effectively.

There is evidence of consistent community outreach, as well as efforts to improve cross-functional (inter-department) communication and coordination. There is also a thorough understanding and compliance with Quality Assurance/Quality Control (QA/QC) throughout the staff. Leaders in the FM organization participate actively in outside professional and technical associations and encourage staff to do the same. Active participation encourages an understanding of FM trends, networking and best practices in the profession.

Strategic & Operational Planning: Leaders of the FM organization develop strategies and plans that are consistent, clear, and well thought out. Strategic goals, objectives, and tactical initiatives are aligned to support the mission of the parent organization. The goals are well understood by department directors, managers and supervisors throughout the organization. The strategic plans are well-documented, tracked, measured and tied to improvement of Facility Management services.

The facilities organization is adequately staffed in terms of levels, skills, and organizational capabilities to meet the needs of the parent organization.

FM leaders have effective operations and capital planning processes in place to develop accurate, prioritized, justifiable and sufficient budgets to operate and maintain the school facilities to the desired level of service. There are effective emergency preparedness and disaster recovery plans, safety and security policies, and communications planning processes. Frequent cross-functional meetings are held to enable effective planning and communication in an integrated fashion. There are clear, documented, and well-coordinated plans for work and asset management. There is also strong collaboration between design and FM staff to ensure sustainable facilities.

Customer Focus: The FM organization has developed a superior service attitude that goes above and beyond for customers. They have proactive processes designed to establish strong relationships and high levels of trust between FM staff and key stakeholders. The FM organization focuses on responsiveness, quality of workmanship, cleanliness, on-site supervisor time with frequent customer contact, proactive identification of work and timely resolution, and professional communication.

The organization's senior-level managers conduct routine visits to proactively solicit feedback and verify service level expectations. There is a centralized work management center (or process) in which the processing of service requests and the execution of work is effectively managed. Customers know how to communicate needs and request work, as well as the full range of facility services provided. There are also comprehensive safety and security programs in place with effective communication to update customers as appropriate.

The proactive customer service program helps optimize the price/quality ratio of facility services. Frequent and consistent communication with customers (e.g., email blasts, newsletters, annual reports, customer satisfaction survey results, project updates, and upcoming events) is carefully managed to keep customers abreast of important initiatives without burdening them with too much information. Facility Management Service Level Agreements (SLAs) have been developed, documented, and communicated for all relevant facilities services.

Maintenance Processes: The FM organization is well organized to effectively and efficiently operate and maintain the facilities. Maintenance policies, practices and procedures are clearly documented and distributed to FM staff and key stakeholders. The process documents include: workflow process maps, maintenance service levels, Operation & Maintenance (O&M) manuals, performance metrics, and other documentation in readily accessible, electronic, easy-to-use, and comprehensive formats.

Work management processes are optimized based on historical and trended data. The processes promote proactive maintenance procedures through proper status code designations and staff incentives. There are complete and accurate equipment/asset inventories for all major maintainable assets that include identification means such as barcodes or Radio Frequency IDentifiers (RFID). Inventory nomenclature and structures follow industry standards such as OmniClass, MasterFormat, Uniformat, and/or COBie (Construction Operations Building Information Exchange) to create confidence in credible facilities data. Parent child relationships and nesting of building systems and equipment and adequate attributes are well defined to enable easy identification of required data, as well as to optimize routing of work.

Proactive maintenance principles are the norm and include robust Preventative Maintenance (PM) and/or Reliability-Centered Maintenance (RCM) programs. The proactive maintenance includes the incorporation of Predictive Testing and Inspection (PT&I), Root Cause Failure Analysis (RCFA), integration with building automation system processes, and automated fault detection and diagnostics. Key metrics include achieving targets of 70 to 80 percent planned maintenance to 20 to 30 percent corrective (i.e., reactive), 90-100% PM completion rates, high percentage of failures addressed using RCFA, high equipment availability/uptime and reliability, measured staff utilization, and Overall Craft Effectiveness (OCE).

FM technologies such as Computerized Maintenance Management Systems (CMMS) or Integrated Work Management Systems (IWMS) are effectively used to support O&M processes, provide accurate data for decision making, and to measure O&M performance. The use of technologies includes ongoing training to align O&M initiatives with the mission, increase the understanding of workflow processes, and enhance the use of the technologies. There is adequate disaster recovery for the supporting technologies and historical data. The maintenance processes are also supported by effective and practical application of hand-held devices.

The maintenance groups consistently monitor trends and incorporate best practices in the maintenance program. This may include standards and processes such as BIM, (Building Information Modeling) COBie and optimized FM technology dashboards.

Operational Processes: Operational services have been well defined, aligned with the mission, and documented in a roles and responsibility matrix of facilities services. Procurement procedures are well documented, including contract administration and inspection procedures, and consistently followed. The FM organization maintains a list of all FM contracts and tracks expiration dates. The FM and procurement organizations meet on a regular basis to review contracts and discuss/update procurement procedures.

Housekeeping and grounds tasks are being performed according to a written, repeatable plan (i.e., internal Service Level Agreement – SLA). A written quality assurance program is in-place and followed. Service levels have been defined and services are measured against the targets. Service levels have been communicated to customers and agreement of expectations and service delivery has been achieved. Key performance indicators or metrics for custodial and grounds are regularly tracked and reported.

Building and building system operations are documented and refined to optimize performance. A clear understanding of the customer's needs and use of the facilities helps operators maximize the performance of building systems. Robust energy and sustainability programs are in place and reported to customers. Energy audits are regularly scheduled and conducted. Energy consumption is tracked and reduced every year. There is an individual responsible for these programs who stays informed about energy conservation trends and conservation.

Workforce Development: There are high levels of competence throughout the FM organization with a lot of pride working for the facilities organization. The competence includes both individual skills and organizational capabilities aligned with the organization's strategy and integrated across service groups. Job position descriptions, roles, and responsibilities within the organization are well-defined. There is a plan and encouragement for ongoing, formal and documented training for technical trades and required credentials/certifications/licenses. There is also a standard employee performance evaluation process on an annual basis in accordance with Human Resources policies and practices. There are opportunities to improve mechanisms for employee feedback and goal setting that is truly linked to the strategy of FM organization and the parent organization.

FM leaders provide clear performance measures, training employees to do their jobs, and enabling employees to work together. They also promote the organization as a good place to work. FM employees are enabled to use their skills, knowledge, and experience to create unique solutions for their customers.

Measurement, Analysis, and Knowledge Management: There is a well-defined and well-communicated level of service and recognition of processes to measure facilities

29

performance. Customer expectations are proactively identified and mapped to a Balanced ScoreCard (BSC) and Key Performance Indicators (KPIs). Use of the BSC is aligned with the mission, the FM strategy map and includes a broad mix of KPI's, including inputs, processes, and output measures. There are well documented processes for performance measurement and data collection to support accurate measurement and knowledge management. The facilities data is routinely reviewed and analyzed to identify trends in performance and needs for continuous improvement.

There is buy-in from all facilities staff on the importance of collecting and managing facilities data to enable performance measurement and benchmarking. There is also commitment to formal quality assurance program and confidence in all levels of the data.

There are procedures in place to periodically benchmark performance with peer organizations. Use of automated benchmarking systems, such as FM Benchmarking, APPA's Facility Performance Indicators database, IFMA's Benchmarking Exchange (Bex), fmDiagnostics™, or other similar systems is employed. There is great confidence in accurate and consistent data, trended over time, to produce creditable and repeatable use of data for O&M process improvement.

Preparing Your Team

To thrive in the current economic and global environment, an organization must have the ability to undertake evolutionary changes. Organizations must have the ability to envision the possibilities and to develop strategies and action plans to realize their full potential. According to Isaac Asimov, *"Scientific fiction is important because it fights the natural notion that there's something permanent about things as they are now"*. We know instinctively there are few things in life that are permanent and change is inevitable, which can be a good thing. So how do you and your FM, team evolve better understand where you are and where you want to be? Many Facility Managers use a basic benchmarking program to evaluate where they are today which is a great start. However, pure benchmarking without attention to process and adoption of change has the potential to fail.

The key to morphing into a high performance organization starts with measuring current conditions and then setting the plan in place to improve. But nothing can take place unless the team is in alignment, motivated to make changes to improve and are empowered and educated. Ultimately, the goal will be reached when the FM team can stimulate creativity, minimize complacency, align the business strategies to action plans and create a sense of ownership in the operations.

Whatever your management approach, the first step of the expedition is the awakening or discovery of what you are doing and how you are doing it. Next, you must compare or benchmark to the best. This can be best achieved with a supported self-evaluation assessment process. What I mean here is that you need experts (internal and external) guiding your path but you and your FM team will need to do the hard work.

In order to implement a cultural shift in how we look at improving through self-evaluation we must create a team dynamic which encourages change in order to thrive and not just survive. Most likely this will begin with change management. There are a variety of ways to approach the team to embrace change. However, first you must understand how your managers look at change in order to facilitate adaptation of new processes and programs to reach true operational excellence.

1. Optimizers: These managers are not interested in major changes but are comfortable with current strategies to reduce costs and enhance the efficiency of existing systems.

2. Reactors: These managers prefer to use existing strategies and react to any changes that occur in the environment in order to improve programs or system efficiency.

3. Forecasters: These managers are preoccupied with identifying what may happen next. They are less concerned about what needs to occur today to deliver better value.

4. Creators: These managers use the knowledge gained by the Forecasters and design new products and services to meet the needs of key stakeholders. They do not make a serious attempt to consider existing processes and to concentrate their efforts in drastically altering them.

It is the opinion of the authors that it takes a mixture of these to create a balanced approach. It is imperative if you are to achieve true operational excellence you must respect those existing strategies (1) which are still applicable if they are in alignment with the new goals. Creator (4) style managers take in information gathered from others to drive progress and change. However, show caution if they completely disregard what is good today which can be built upon. Which style are you? For an organization to experience success for both today and in the foreseeable future, it requires managers who can simultaneously juggle different structures and cultures. A greater understanding and appreciation of how these structures and styles function will help you in adapting and moving the change in culture and operations to be successful.

Those who are trying to achieve organization or team evolution need to keep in mind how people change by learning. As part of individual learning, we have professional intellect. Quinn, Anderson, and Finkelstein (1996) have identified four levels of professional intellect:

1. Know-what: the basic cognitive knowledge to perform a task
2. Know-how: the skills needed to apply the knowledge in actual problems
3. Know-why: the knowledge of overall organizational culture, politics, key players, and of how to interact with those elements to accomplish the task at hand
4. Care-why: the will to be highly motivated and adaptive

Each level is a prerequisite to the next and an organization must attain the *"care-why"* level before innovative change can take place. It is up to you as the change agent perhaps to create the training and or communication plan to take your organization all the way from knowing what needs to be done to caring that it get accomplished at the highest level. Organizations that nurture the *"care-why"* in their people can truly thrive in the face of today's rapid changing pace and reach the desired summit.

So what does that mean for you as a Facility Management professional? While the FM profession has come a long way, visionary leadership and creative business practices are required for you to create a high performance FM organization. In order to utilize a process such as fmDiagnostics™, the FM team must be open to a possible culture shift. It requires the staff and leadership to be open and communicative which can be challenging for some. There are proven methods to achieving this type of growth within your organization.

The following are seven skillsets which must be developed within your FM team in order to build a high performance FM organization:

1. Leadership & Business Skills

Facilities Management is becoming more and more an important business element for organizations as the costs of real estate increase and the impact of the built environment on productivity of employees becomes more and more recognized.

Whether your department is considered tactical or strategic it is important for you to demonstrate to the organization that Facilities Management isn't just about maintenance or office moves, it has an impact on the organization's results.

This is where leadership and business skills become more important than technical skills when you are leading your Facility department. You are competing with other department heads and these skills help you get your initiatives implemented and will enable you to make positive changes, not just maintaining the status quo.

2. Skill and Knowledge

At the top of your department, leadership and business skills are important, but your organization still needs to be knowledge based. With the complexity of FM, you need to either have staff with key facilities skills or you need to be able to access them through consultants or contractors. Even if you are a department of one, you can't know everything you need to know. The skill of a manager and leader is to know where to get the skills and knowledge they need when they need it. When looking for resources with the skills, choose people who keep up with the latest approaches and trends and have an open mind for change.

In addition, to being a leader for your organization, you need to seek out additional knowledge from other sources. That means active involvement in associations where you can attend and learn from conferences, including the trade show floor where new products and solutions can be found. Networking within the industry is imperative as it multiplies your resources considerably. This enables you to pick up the phone or send a note asking others if they have a solution to a problem that is new to you.

3. **Policies and Procedures for All Functions**

Managing facilities is a process and services based profession. A leading organization does what they do consistently in a way that is both efficient and effective. The best way to achieve operational success is to have well developed and communicated procedures which guide staff, suppliers and even occupants through the steps and requirements of FM function. Some of the things you should have in place include:

- **Asset Management** – Regularly review property condition using formal process checklists. Integrate the results from this and your maintenance management system into your capital and maintenance plans.
- **Communications** – Use newsletters, emails, meetings, etc. in a planned and controlled way to communicate and receive communication from occupants.
- **Customer Service** – Have policies and procedures in place to deal with customer/occupant communications and issues. Measure satisfaction results, develop corrective action plans and implement them.

- **Emergency Management** – Well defined written plans for dealing with emergencies and issues, including disasters, accidents and business recovery.
- **Energy Management** – Actively managing energy through formal plans and initiatives.
- **Environmental Management** – Written plans that address all environmental issues such as CFC's, hazardous waste, spills, fluorescent tubes, etc. to be reducing impacts.
- **General Management** – You develop annual plans to address issues, set initiatives and targets, including facility plans, asset and capital plans, staff training, communications, etc.
- **Lease Management** – You have formal processes and resources to scrutinize lease charges from landlords and property tax.
- **Maintenance Management** – You have a computerized system that tracks assets, plans preventive maintenance, tracks corrective maintenance and demand work orders and provides reporting for management, compliance and performance.
- **Occupancy Management** – You have systems to track, analyze and report usage to provide management and strategic information for cost containment and planning to drive behaviors and reduce total cost of ownership/occupancy.
- **Performance Management** – You have quantifiable measurements of key deliverables and processes for suppliers and in-house staff.

You have a normal process and measurement framework that drives improvements.

- **Quality Assurance** – You have a formal quality assurance process in place that ensures consistent processes and procedures, results are monitored and compliance audits performed. Mechanisms are in place for continuous improvement.
- **Staff Development** – You annually review, recommend and implement training for your team to stay current and develop your staff. You participate in associations and subscribe to related publications to stay current in the industry.
- **Standards** – You have standards to minimize costs and ensure consistency for space layouts, furniture, fit-up and capital or base-building projects.

This also enables you to manage activities better, implement quality assurance, audit processes, have training tools for staff, both new and existing, and review performance with employees.

4. Information Analysis and Decision Making

You can't manage what you don't know, and you can't make effective decisions without information. A high performing organization has Facilities Management software at a minimum to manage the help desk, preventive and demand maintenance and work orders and space management, including moves. This includes CMMS, CAFM (Computer-Aided Facility Management), IWMS, etc.

Just having a system isn't enough however, you need to effectively collect and use the data from your systems and turn it into information you can use for decisions. This means analyzing the data and information, which usually requires more sophisticated analysis reports from your system.

Even better, export the data, or parts of the data, into Excel where you can analyze it. The end result in gathering data is to compare different elements such as number of complaints by floor, department, staff, month of the year, service provider, etc.

Looking at trends within your internal benchmarking is the best way to use information to decide what is working, what doesn't and what needs to be changed. It can give you the critical information to build a business case for senior management when you request a revenue or resource driven operational change.

5. Customer Service Awareness

By providing internal customer service, you are enabling your organization's core business and improving its chance for success.

High performing FM departments think about customer service not as something that just needs to be done, but is something which is important to your organization's success. It's not just about the smiles or quick service, it's about delivering what your customers at all levels, from staff sitting at their desk to department managers and to the CEO need to be successful.

Great customer service involves implementing processes that ensure the necessary service is delivered consistently by your team, including staff and service

38

providers (level 3 on the CMM–Capability Maturity Model). But more than that, it needs systems that can enable your team to adjust delivery when the unique situation requires it, to identify problems that need to be rectified and enable quick escalation in rectification of service issues (level 4 on CMM).

Consistent measurement of your internal customer's satisfaction with your service is imperative. Your FM team needs detailed information about every aspect of your service delivery that will help you meet expectations or deliver the service organization needs. Surveys may include occupant surveys, decision-maker surveys and transaction surveys. One word of caution here, take care to only ask questions or solicit feedback on issues that you can actually impact otherwise you set yourself up for failure. Remember to not over promise and under deliver by giving unrealistic expectations of capabilities.

6. Quality Assurance

The foundation of any good FM organization is its ability to measure quality and adjust its processes to maintain the quality required and possible for the organization. Quality standards must be appropriate for the budget and capabilities of the FM group. Do not set yourself up for failure while you are stretching to reach a new goal or standard. You should implement a quality assurance program that includes processes, audits, quality control, continuous reviews, analysis and action plans. It is best to gain concurrence from the team in the beginning and then implement a training program for your staff and service providers alike.

Quality control (an inspection program) is only the beginning. Quality assurance is a proactive approach to ensure that when you do your inspection you're more likely to achieve the KPI's or benchmarks you set.

As part of the proactive nature of quality assurance, it should include a review of the processes to ensure they are achieving the results you expect. Keep the balance of the level and quality of service you're delivering with what is required by the organization and departments you serve. Do not over or under serve your customers.

7.   Forward Leaning Solutions

In the past, Facilities Management was mostly reactive, behind the scenes function. However the profession has evolved and expectations have evolved. Instead of simply being the maintenance department or the office admin group, (mops & cops & walls & halls) what you do has an increasingly important impact on the organization's costs and productivity. Facilities costs for an organization are typically the second or third largest expense line. The largest expense line is usually personnel costs, which are impacted by the work environment you manage.

This requires a forward leaning or proactive approach to issues and problems. So as part of your role, you should become much more educated and aware of the impact of the physical work environment on employee productivity, morale and retention. Thus the importance of staying connected to professional associations and strong networking. This awareness of the industry offerings will better enable you when evaluating your current operations against documented best practices3.

Your organization has a direct impact and you can support other departments in these areas where they are driven from facilities issues. You must have a seat at the decision table with your   senior management in your organization regarding future plans, growth etc. This will allow you to be proactive in identifying and developing options, alternatives and flexibility to meet your organization's plans before they are even implemented. By creating what-if scenarios with opportunities and risks, senior management will see you as being proactive. Thus, you can enable the organizations goals and objectives rather than simply responding to them.

[3] Theriault, Michel. Managing Facilities & Real Estate. WoodStone Press, 2010

Chapter 3: FM Evaluation & Improvement Tools

Of all the organizational assessment tools and protocols we have evaluated, we selected the best components of each to refine our organizational diagnostics approach. fmDiagnostics™ is a standardized Facility Management organization and process evaluation system. It is the first true comprehensive organizational and leadership diagnostic tool developed specifically to measure FM performance and assist in creating high performance facilities organizations.

Approach & Methodology

The systems approach to FM evaluations incorporated into fmDiagnostics™ is based on best practices, benchmarks, and standards published by IFMA, APPA, and the NRC/FFC. fmDiagnostics™ also employs leadership assessment processes developed at the Harvard Business School (the Balanced ScoreCard) and the Baldrige National Quality Program (BNQP) quality measurement system. The methodology also incorporates the structure of the capabilities maturity model to identify maturity/capability levels of an FM organization.

The Baldrige National Quality Program (BNQP) criteria for performance excellence include:

[A] Leadership
[B] Strategic and Operational Planning
[C] Customer Focus
[D] Measurement, Analysis, and Knowledge Management
[E] Workforce Focus and Development
[F] Process Management
[G] Performance Results

These categories map to IFMA core competencies as follows:

1. Leadership and Strategy – [A], [B] and [C]
2. O&M Management – [F]
3. Project Management – [F]
4. Business and Finance – [D]
5. Real Estate – [F]
6. Human and Environmental Factors – [E], [C] and [F]
7. Communication – [A] and [F]
8. Technology – [F] and [D]
9. Quality Assessment and Innovation – [C], [D] and [G]
10. Environmental Stewardship & Sustainability – [A], [B], [D] and [F]
11. Emergency Preparedness – [B] and [F]

A standardized question set based on experience of FM core processes and best practices, IMFA core competencies, APPA's body of knowledge, and the NRC framework of essential areas of expertise was developed to provide the foundation of the tool. The question set is categorized by Baldrige performance areas, weighted and linked to an organizational capability maturity level (refer to Figure 5) based on the responses to the questions.

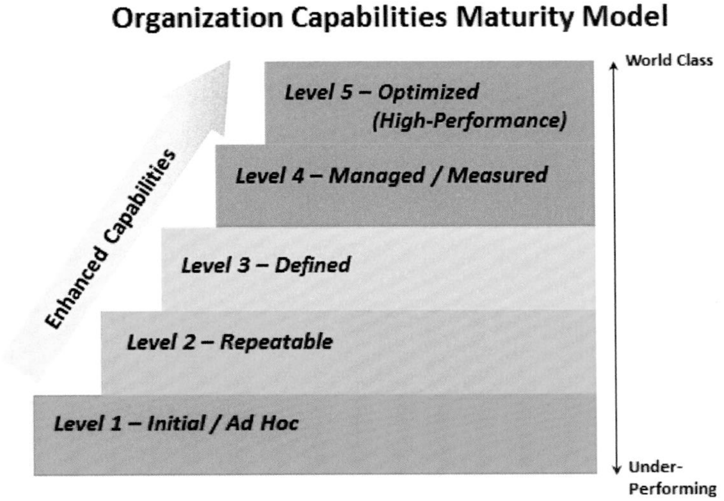

Organization Capabilities Maturity Model

Figure 5: Capabilities Maturity Levels

Process Improvement

fmDiagnostics™ is more than simply a benchmarking tool. It goes beyond benchmarking best practices to expertly diagnose FM operational issues, recommend cures, prescribe long-term solutions, and provide a simple means of monitoring improved organizational health. The systems approach focuses on FM performance excellence by evaluating the entire organization in an overall management framework to identify strengths and opportunities for improvement.

The real value of fmDiagnostics™ is that it is a comprehensive approach to support not just the evaluation of FM performance, but to aid in providing recommendations for process improvement. Each question (over 150) listed in the fmDiagnostics™ database has a corresponding '*more information*' tab that describes why the element is important to achieving success.

Each element also has a corresponding recommendation to take action upon and improve performance.

We created an approach to prioritize recommendations and help clients sequence actions over time. One of the most favored tools included our recommendation impact/effort quad chart. This graph plots recommendations with respect to the level of effort anticipated to implement the recommendation (including our opinion of labor, tools, and contracted costs) versus the level of potential impact to the organization. The impact to the organization is difficult to discretely define and can include quantifiable savings, qualitative value aspects, and other intangible benefits.

Benefits/Value

Just as individuals can benefit significantly from getting routine health checkups, fmDiagnostics™ was developed to measure the health of a facilities organization. Much like standard human health predictors, such as weight, cholesterol, blood pressure, etc., fmDiagnostics™ uses a pre-defined set of organizational health indicators to measure the short- and long-term health of an organization and present recommendations to improve performance Creating a high performance FM organization will help:

- Fully support the corporation's strategic business initiatives
- Enhance operational efficiencies and effectiveness
- Reduce costs both short-term and long-term
- Optimize process performance through scheduled and methodical process review and identified modifications
- Maximize Return-On-Investment (ROI) with prioritized vetted decisions
- Minimize Total Cost of Ownership (TCO)
- Maximize asset value and life cycle
- Continuously monitor improved performance

- Build pride in the FM organization to enhance attracting and retaining of quality employees throughout the organization

fmDiagnostics™ is not simply a benchmarking tool. It goes beyond benchmarking best practices to expertly diagnose FM operational issues, recommend cures, prescribe long-term solutions, and provide a simple means of monitoring improved organizational health. The systems approach focuses on FM performance excellence by evaluating the entire organization in an overall management framework to identify strengths and opportunities for improvement.

Key Performance Indicators (KPIs) are identified and developed early on in the process and formulated into a balanced scorecard for the FM organization. Evaluation scores are developed for each area and process and linked to the scorecard KPIs. This enables measuring improvements of scores integrated directly with benefits (such as cost avoidance, energy conservation, extended asset life, higher customer productivity and satisfaction, minimized risk, and other tangible benefits). The system is completely transparent to stakeholders. It was developed based on the tenants of using a rational approach and recognizable standards to generate credible and repeatable results.

The fmDiagnostics™ Difference

Many current FM assessment tools used today are based on quality measurement systems designed to measure product quality and improve process engineering. These measurement systems include Top Quality Management (TQM), Six Sigma, ISO, and BNQP. TQM and Six Sigma systems generally concentrate on driving process improvement to increase product quality and generate cost savings. ISO 9001:2000 Registration is a product conformity model for guaranteeing equity in the marketplace. ISO, like Six Sigma, also focuses on fixing quality defects and product non-conformities. While some of the concepts are valid for facilities organizations, fmDiagnostics™ differs as it is specific to FM operations including supporting the leadership, the focus on customer satisfaction and FM process monitoring and management, all leading to exceptional FM performance results.

Specific and compatible aspects of top quality measurement systems are incorporated into fmDiagnostics™ systems approach. What fmDiagnostics™ does, that other assessment approaches don't, is to integrate recognized quality standards for FM services with a repeatable and transparent scoring system linked to KPIs aligned with the organization's strategy. This makes it very effective to implement improvements aligned with the mission/vision of the organization, and accurately measure the results.

Rating performance does not need to be an exercise in subjectivity and personal bias. If the right performance indicators are developed with an eye toward measurability, a performance rating system can be developed for each of the categories that define high performance. The Balanced ScoreCard (BSC) is a performance management tool that allows the Facility Manager to develop initiatives, measures, and targets that are used to measure success around *all* of the elements of the performance management framework. The BSC bridges the gap between the organizational strategy and the delivery of a high performance Facility Management organization. Once the framework is in place, continuous measurement and quantification of success will start to define high performance at the organizational level.

Not everyone is convinced that all things are measurable. However, using similar techniques to that of how we measure customer satisfaction, we can make subjective evaluations more objective, and we can develop rating systems for characteristics such as the strength of our leadership, ability to develop our workforce, and the measurement and analysis process we implement.

Chapter 4: fmDiagnostics™ Components

fmD follows the framework established by Baldrige and incorporates seven performance categories: leadership, strategic and operational planning, customer focus, workforce development, maintenance, operations and measurement, analysis and knowledge management. Each of the modules is defined below.

fmDiagnostics™ Framework

Leadership: Leadership is guiding and directing others actions and decisions through personal influence and power. Effective leaders will channel the energy of others to help support the achievement of an organization's goals (IFMA 2010b). *"Leadership ensures that the FM organization is motivated to move down the right path"* (IFMA 2010b).

Strategic and Operational Planning: Day to day operational plans should be developed based on strategic plans using a well-developed strategy. Strategy is the science of the planning process that uses a program of action to reach a goal. Strategy focuses on the big picture and long-term needs of the organization (IFMA 2010b). A strategic plan defines the missions, vision, values, goals and resources of an organization. A strategic plan should describe how an organization intends to create value to its stakeholders (IFMA 2010b). The plan should also document how the organization will respond to both internal and external factors. External factors may include economic, political and social concerns. Internal factors may include talent pool, organizational culture and the availability of resources.

Operational planning includes the plans necessary to define how the facility will be operated on a day to day basis to meet the needs of the customer. Examples of operational plans include Standard Operating Procedures (SOPs), the asset management plans, and the Facility Condition Assessments (FCAs).

Customer Focus: Customer focus is how an organization determines the needs of the customer and takes action to satisfy them (IFMA 2012). This requires interacting with the customer. A customer is a person who uses and/or receives services from the Facility Management organization. A few examples of interaction are an HVAC technician responding to a hot/cold call, the Facility Manager speaking with the management officer about the need to find a chiller repair or Facility Management staff discussing how to solve a safety concern with a hired contractor.

Workforce Focus and Development: A workforce is a group of workers hired to provide a defined set of responsibilities to an organization. Workforce focus and development requires allocating proper time to understand the skill sets required to properly operate and maintain a facility. More specifically, this means defining core competencies and developing a strategy so that the Facility Management organization as a team has the skills necessary to meet the needs of the overall organization. One resource to help federal facility teams define core competencies and develop strategies is the Federal Buildings Personnel Training Act (FBPTA).

It should be recognized that workforce focus should be team focused, opposed to individual employee focused. A single individual will never have all of the skills or capacity to meet all of the needs of a facilities organization. Thus, it is important to differentiate between individual skills and team skills. For example, in a three person team, one person may be very effective at general management; the second person is an effective writer and the third person an effective communicator with the customer. The skill set of these three individuals should be leveraged so that the workload is balanced and the team is using the strengths of each team member.

Process Management – Maintenance: Maintenance is the processes and procedures necessary to make sure that building infrastructure is serviced to operate efficiently, reliability and safely. It includes scheduling and completing regularly scheduled maintenance, and using a balance of preventive, predictive and corrective maintenance practices.

Process Management – Operations: Operations is the processes and procedures necessary to make sure the facility and how it is used provides a satisfactory work environment that is in compliance with laws and regulations, meets financial performance goals, uses utilities in an efficient and cost effective manner and protects the surrounding environment.

Measurement, Analysis and Knowledge Management: This module includes three interrelated topics. Measurements are necessary to complete analysis. Knowledge management is necessary to keep measurements and analysis findings organized and to determine how to effectively use this information to meet the needs of the FM organization and the customer.

Measurement is a quantitative value that expresses the size, frequency of an event, amount, degree of satisfaction or other measure to help the Facility Management team make data driven decisions. Measurements can take many forms, ranging from automated readings from sensors or meters, manual readings from valves and gages and customer satisfaction surveys. Thus, measurement within Facility Management is not an exact science: measurements can be *"moving targets"* and often are impacted by humans, and only represent a snapshot in time. The measurement process requires the collection of both qualitative and quantitative data. Measurements of past performance, such as historical data, are important to help avoid past mistakes. However, strategic and future-focused measures are equally important to advance the mission, vision and values of the FM organization.

As a part of the assessment, a series of questions have been designed specifically for each of these performance areas. A series of sub-modules (topics) have also been identified for each module with specific questions. They include:

- Leadership
  - Communication
  - Effective Organizational Structure
  - Effective and Documented Processes
  - Quality Improvement
  - FM Trends and Professional Networking
- Strategic and Operational Planning
  - Plans
  - Communication Plans
  - Planning Implementation
  - Safety/Environmental Plans
  - Facility Designs
- Customer Focus
  - Customer Input and Feedback
  - Work Control
  - Safety and Security
  - New Employees

- o O&M Manual
- Workforce Focus and Development
  - o Employee Job Descriptions and Succession Planning
  - o Training and Professional Development (PD)
  - o Employee Recognition and Rewards
  - o Employee Performance and Feedback
- Process Part 1 – Maintenance
  - o Documentation
  - o Work Management and Work Orders
  - o Asset and Equipment Inventory Program
  - o Automated Work Management System
  - o Preventive Maintenance (PM)
- Process Part 2 – Operations
  - o Service Levels
  - o Procurement procedures
  - o Custodial Services
  - o Ground Management
  - o Energy Management, Utilities, and Sustainability Program
  - o Environmental Health and Safety
  - o Regulatory Compliance
  - o Space Management
  - o Lease Management
  - o Project and Construction Management Program
  - o Relocation & Moves/Add/Changes
- Measurement, Analysis, and Knowledge Management
  - o Defined Level of Service (LOS)
  - o Process to Evaluate Organizational Performance
  - o Balanced and Flexible KPIs
  - o FM Organizational Benchmarking

Organizational Capability Maturity Models (CMM)

Continued experience with evaluations and feedback from clients has led to further development of the fmDiagnostics™ reporting structure. While the scoring has proved beneficial, we have improved fmDiagnostics™ by incorporating a capability maturity model framework to provide a better path for organizational improvement. Positive findings in our research of organizational capability maturity models led to efforts to restructure our approach and reporting structure. We believe there will be significant benefit to FM organizations with a new format to the questions and outcomes enabling better alignment to the levels of organization capability maturity.

Benchmarking / Performance Measures

The earliest development stages of fmDiagnostics™ included a methodology to score each performance area defined in the Baldrige framework. This enabled FEA to focus and report on opportunities for improvement in each of the key areas. Key Performance Indicators (KPIs) can be identified and developed early on in the process and formulated into a balanced scorecard for the FM organization. Evaluation scores should be linked to each area and process and identified into the scorecard KPIs. This enables the measuring of improvements and the scores to be aligned directly with benefits (such as cost avoidance, energy conservation, extended asset life, higher customer productivity and satisfaction, minimized risk, and other tangible benefits).

The system is completely transparent to stakeholders. It was developed based on the tenants of using a rational approach and recognizable standards to generate credible and repeatable results. This can result in verifiable evidence based improvements. This becomes a validation to document change and can support your requests of labor, money or other needed resources.

Results

Results are all about planting the flag at the summit, telling the FM story, and proving you are a world class facilities organization. We need to improve our ability in not only predicting outcomes of facilities operations and maintenance, but measuring performance as well.

FM organizations are challenged with providing support services to multiple customers in the most cost-effective and productive manner possible. Effective and efficient programs help determine how well the parent organization will meet its mission. In support of the organization's goals, the facilities organization is tasked with developing effective facilities operations and maintenance programs to provide safe, productive, and clean environments where people can conduct their business. This is the launching pad for the development of specific objectives, strategies, and tactics to be able to execute the mission and truly measure performance.

Based on the goals and objectives set forth by an organization, the FM leadership should prepare a FM Strategy Map and related key performance indicators. The FM Strategy Map organizes the FM objectives in a balanced scorecard framework. An example may include: 1) Delivering exceptional customer service, 2) Being respected as stewards of the physical environment, 3) Providing a safe and rewarding working environment, and 4) Focusing on teamwork, innovation, and professionalism.

The final step is to develop actions/tactics for each objective and strategies with corresponding measurements and targets. As a launching point, we recommend considering over a broad array of potential metrics based on industry standards, but specific to the objectives and strategies of the FM organization. From here we recommend selecting the top ten KPIs to report up to FM and the parent organization stakeholders. These KPIs are directly linked to the facilities strategic plan and to the balanced scorecard.

The best facilities management organizations have tremendous focus. This focus can be achieved by establishing specific objectives and measures that drive strategy-specific actions. It is critical to realize four vital elements:

- **Focus** – Many facilities identify too many metrics. Focus on what is essential for success, not what is easy to measure.
- **Validity** – Evaluate and measure specifics, not intangibles like values, teamwork, partnerships, etc. and focus on validating outcomes, not inputs.
- **Connectivity** – Use measures that connect managers/leaders to their scorecard in ways that they can understand and influence.
- **Integration** – The performance measures must be integrated, not only into your FM technology, but into the organization's performance management practices, or it will not change employee behavior.

The framework set by the balanced scorecard approach provides an excellent methodology to measure overall performance as facilities managers. The balanced scorecard approach dissects an organization and its influencing factors, or perspectives. Specifically, the balanced scorecard approach asks an organization to look at operations from four different perspectives.

- **Customer Perspective Metrics** – Customer Satisfaction Surveys, Work Order Response Time, Percent Return Work, Cleanliness / Aesthetics, Comfort & Safety (e.g., Hot-Cold Calls), Communication.

- **Employee Perspective Metrics** – Employee Assessment Surveys, Employee Turnover Rate, Productivity (Wrench-turning Time), Annual Training Hours, WO's Generated by inspections, On-Site Supervisor Time.

- **Process Perspective Metrics** – PM vs. CM Ratio, PM Completion Rates, WO Turn-Around Time (Aging), Unscheduled Downtime/Root Cause Analysis, Mean Time Between Failures (MTBF), Maintenance OT Percentage.

- **Financial Perspective Metrics** – Capital Renewal as % of CRV, Operating Costs as % of CRV, FCI (DM / CRV), Maintenance Cost vs. Replacement Cost, Site Utility Index, Facility Maintenance Costs per S.F.

While the framework is there, it is not always easy to implement the right metrics to achieve a successful scorecard. The problem lies not in a lack of understanding of the models, but in a number of contributing factors. These factors include: a lack of focus on measuring what is needed instead of what is easy to measure, measuring too many activities and not focusing on the outcomes, the sheer number of inter-related variables that affect performance, not effectively using complex FM technologies IWMS and ERPs (Enterprise Resource Planning) to capture the right information, getting commitment from facilities stakeholders and staff to capture the right data, and finally, overcoming the fear of consequences of measuring performance.

The true value of the balanced scorecard approach is that it allows managers to link the strategy of the FM organization to execution of work. As previously mentioned, the important aspect is to link the execution of FM processes and workflow to strategy. It is important to at least be aware of this plan and how it links the strategy to day-to-day work. Supervisors and managers must be more familiar with the objectives and actions to effectively implement change and improvements.

Chapter 5: Case Studies

Facility Engineering Associates (FEA) has conducted hundreds of assessments across different industry domains. We offer two of them in this chapter to provide real life examples of the benefits of the application fmDiagnostics™.

Case Study #1 – IT Domain

FEA conducted a facilities management evaluation of the Department of Facilities for an educational institution using our fmDiagnostics™ process. FEA focused on the organization, processes, technologies, and metrics using objective criteria developed as part of fmDiagnostics™. The purpose of the evaluation was to support the vision of the institution's FM leaders *"to identify opportunities for projects that take advantage of additional proven technologies thus enhancing the efficiency of the FM organization"*. These projects addressed both technology and process enhancements that provided a measurable return on investment while improving the quantity of data available to the organization.

Overall, the Facilities Department was well organized and has developed processes that were strategically aligned to help achieve its mission of advancing knowledge and educating students in science, technology, and other areas of scholarship that will best serve the nation and the world in the 21st century. There was a high degree of technical and managerial competence and apparent high levels of trust both within the organization and of the organization by Facilities Department customers. We noted a high level of customer service and maintenance response with respect to limited O&M staffing levels (validated by benchmark reports). While the O&M organization has done a good job in maintaining reliability of the building systems through the prioritization of work and resources, the combination of aging and complex buildings and restricted maintenance has led to a high backlog of deferred maintenance.

Other accomplishments noted include a broad, accepted and effective use of the Facility Management information technologies (CMMS/IWMS). Support of the Integrated Work Management System (IWMS) was provided by capable staff, but again with very limited staff resources. There was also effective consolidation and use of the building automation systems to maintain reliability of service and enhance staff efficiencies. Other facility information systems supported by the FM Department provided leading edge capabilities with respect to mapping, Geographic Information System (GIS), building information models, and document management.

While the IWMS was well used and supported, we did note a lack of data standards and limited use of some functionality that could substantially enhance overall effectiveness and efficiencies of the organization. Implementation of certain data standards would also support opportunities to improve preventive maintenance programs and root cause analysis processes. Key findings identified during our site visits and subsequent interviews are summarized as follows:

- The O&M organization is very lean for the size of the campus. Maintenance is largely reactive due in part to the resource constraints and aging buildings. There is a well-established preventive maintenance program, however, it could benefit from the introduction of technologies such as handheld devices, predictive testing and inspection technologies, and other diagnostic tools.

- One of the biggest challenges the O&M organization faces is the coordination and integration of work across trade shops and campus services teams. There appears to be some lack of understanding of how to best coordinate maintenance activities. Better definition of work roles and integration by documenting and streamlining processes could create efficiencies.

- We identified a need for both overall process and technology training to support both current workflow and enhanced processes. Improved commitment and understanding of both how and why work should be accomplished can be established through an internal training program.

- Finally, there should be more focus on the measurement of key performance indicators aligned with the facilities mission to tell the story of the O&M organization. There is currently limited ability to baseline or track improved performance, thought the tools are available.

Details of key findings, accomplishments and recommendations for initiatives to enhance efficiencies are provided in the following sections. The body of the report contains a prioritization of recommendations.

Summary of Recommendations

Based on our evaluation and findings, we grouped our recommendations into four main categories related to: technologies and tools, workflow processes, performance measurement, and workforce development and training. A listing of the recommendations is summarized as follows.

<u>Technologies and Tools</u>

1. Establish FM Data Standards (e.g., equipment, PM, buildings, rooms)
2. Create IWMS Problem and Repair Codes
3. Link Work Orders to Equipment for Histories
4. Implement Predictive Testing & Inspection (PT&I) Technologies
5. Purchase Other Diagnostic Tools (e.g., trending temperature loggers, controls, etc.)
6. Experiment with Handheld Applications (PM group and stockroom)
7. Test Bar Coding of Equipment for PM
8. Consider Building Automation System (BAS) Upgrades
9. Integrate Graphics and O&M Manuals
10. Develop Dashboards for Supervisors (metrics) – Plasma Displays (situation room) – to show metrics
11. Move to COTS (Commercial-Off-The-Shelf) Space Planning Solution to Support O&M
12. Purchase vehicles for Preventive Maintenance (PM) team

<u>Workflow Processes</u>

13. Work on Supervisor Integration
14. Operations Center and Instrumentation Team Integration
15. HVAC Mechanic / PM Tech / Instrumentation Tech Integration
16. Establish Formal Root Cause Analysis Process (resources)
17. Consider Systems Engineer for BAS Analysis
18. Implement Escalation Process – Reduce Work Order (WO) Aging
19. Document Processes - Defining work better to take away ambiguity and excuses
20. Consider Adding Weekend and Third Shift Supervision
21. Expand Stockroom Hours (i.e. 6 am to 4 pm)

Performance Measurement

22. Establish Metrics (Balanced Scorecard)
23. Invest in FM Technology Metrics and Reports

Workforce Development/Training

24. Develop Long-Term O&M Training Program
25. Experiment with UPK Software
26. Provide Additional Training on Controls

   To help prioritize the recommendations above, we included a chart illustrating (qualitatively), the Level of Effort versus Level of Impact. The chart compares each recommendation, the amount of effort in staff, dollars, and time, and the subsequent positive impact for the Facilities Department organization.

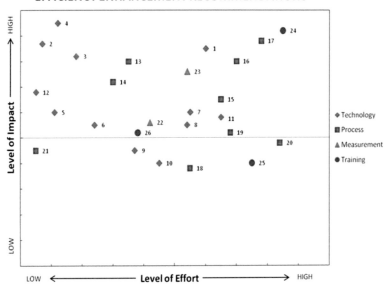

Figure 6: Level of Effort versus Level of Impact

65

The prioritization and order of implementation of some of the recommendations warranted further explanation regarding timeframe and prerequisites. We sorted the 26 recommendations for efficiency improvements into categories of short-, mid-, and long-term. Short-term is defined as one to two years for implementation and payback; mid-term is between two and five years; and long-term is defined as projects that were essentially on-going upgrades and process evolutions.

Short-term Recommendations
Establish SAP (System Application Products) Data Standards
Create SAP Problem and Repair Codes
Implement Predictive Testing & Inspection (PT&I) Technologies
Purchase Other Diagnostic Tools
Purchase Vehicle for PM Team
Establish Formal Root Cause Analysis Process
Document Processes – Defining Work Better
Expand Stockroom Hours (6 am to 4 pm)
Establish Metrics (Balanced Scorecard)
Invest in SAP Reports

Mid-term Recommendations
Link Work Orders to Equipment for Histories
Experiment with Handheld Applications
Test Bar Coding of Equipment for PM

Work on Supervisor Integration
Operations Center and Instrumentation Team Integration
HVAC Mechanic / PM Tech / Instrumentation Tech Integration
Implement Escalation Process – Reduce Work Order (WO) Aging
Consider Adding Weekend and Third Shift Supervision
Develop Long-Term O&M Training Program
Experiment with UPK Software

Long-term Recommendations
Consider Building Automation System (BAS) Upgrades
Integrate Graphics and O&M Manuals (easier meridian access)
Develop Dashboards for Supervisors (metrics)
Move to COTS Space Planning Solution to Support O&M
Consider Systems Engineer for BAS Analysis
Provide Additional Training on Controls

The review team's knowledge and experience as successful practitioners of higher educational facilities management and administration formed the judgment and recommendations of this report. That knowledge and experience was combined with a cursory interview process, document review, and studied comparisons. The judgments and recommendations included in the report were given not by way of criticism, but rather as a means to assist the Facilities Department in its effort to continuously improve efficiency and to better meet the needs of the institution.

Case Study #2 – Public Domain

Facility Engineering Associates (FEA) has conducted dozens of comprehensive facilities management evaluations of Public School System Facilities Management Divisions using the fmDiagnostics™ process. An example of an evaluation of one of the top ten largest school districts in the country is presented herein. FEA evaluated the FM organization, policies, processes, and metrics using seven objective criteria developed as part of fmDiagnostics™. The performance criteria utilized to guide this review included:

- Leadership
- Strategic and Operational Planning
- Customer Satisfaction
- Measurement
- Workforce Development
- O&M Process Management
- Performance Results

Overall, the Public School System (PSS) FM division was well organized and had developed processes that are strategically aligned to help the PSS achieve the goal of providing a safe and nurturing environment which will enable the education of outstanding students. Recent efforts to improve the quality of FM business processes through Six Sigma Lean process improvement initiatives have generated substantial value and cost avoidance. The FM organization operated well above the average public school system across all areas of performance categories (reference Figure 7 below). Areas of potential improvement included: improving documentation of and access to FM policies and procedures, more focus on formalized workforce development and training to create redundancy in staff expertise, and enhancement of performance measurement.

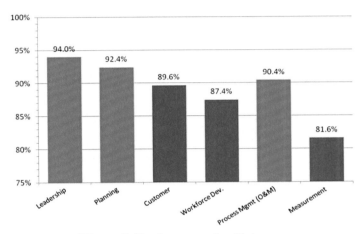

Figure 7: Performance by Category

A summary of key findings, accomplishments and recommendations for improvement are provided in the following sections.

Leadership: In general, the leadership of the FM organization had created a well-organized and functional divisional structure with excellent strategic planning processes and effective communication. There was evidence of consistent community outreach, as well as efforts to improve cross-functional (inter-department) communication and coordination. The FP&M (Facilities Planning & Management) leadership was active in relevant professional networks to monitor trends and best practices. One of the most substantial accomplishments is the implementation of a lean quality process improvement program that has already reaped substantial rewards. Continuation of these practices will lead to a high performing and valuable organization.

Strategic and Operational Planning: FM leaders had created an integrated strategic and operational planning process aligned with the mission of the public school system. There were effective budgeting (both operational and capital), safety and security, and communications planning processes. While there was evidence of uniform operational standards and guidelines, there is room for continued improvement of specifications for construction and maintenance. Two noteworthy accomplishments include the development of a comprehensive maintenance program and a custodial services improvement program developed by the School Facilities Department. Another significant accomplishment was the implementation of Facility Condition Assessments (FCAs) to develop a credible and reliable capital asset management program.

Customer Satisfaction: While we did not interview external FP&M customers for the evaluation, we did note several proactive processes designed to establish strong relationships and high levels of trust between FM staff and school stakeholders. The senior-level managers conducted routine school visits to solicit feedback and verify service level expectations. There was a centralized work management center to expedite the processing of service requests and the execution of work, as well as improving communication with customers. There were also comprehensive safety and security programs in place with effective communication to update school staff as appropriate. Two areas of potential improvement focus on public outreach / customer relations and include: 1) Incorporating FM policies and processes as an integral part of the organization's and school's new employee on-boarding process, and 2) Improving documentation of FP&M policies and procedures for use by school staff.

Workforce Development: There appeared to be a high level of competence throughout the FM organization with a lot of pride working for the school system. Job position descriptions, roles, and responsibilities within the organization were well defined. There was encouragement for ongoing training for technical trades and required certifications. However, the training appeared to be informal, varied by department, did not have specific line-item budgeting, and was not entirely well documented. There was also a standard employee performance evaluation process on an annual basis in accordance with Human Resources policies and practices. There were opportunities to improve mechanisms for employee feedback and goal setting that is truly linked to the strategy of FM and the school system. An encouraging accomplishment is the more recent involvement of senior leaders of the FM organization in the recruiting process to focus on finding and attracting top talent.

O&M Process Management: The performance area of O&M Process Management included the evaluation of the following categories: Workflow processes and documentation, work management and work orders, asset and equipment inventory and management, facility audits and assessments, space management, project and construction management, energy and sustainability management, grounds and custodial services, facility operations and procurement, levels of service, maintenance programs, security and life safety, adherence to applicable laws and regulations, and facilities management technology (automated work and space management).

A well-structured FM organization coupled with efforts to improve processes through lean quality programs had led to the creation of effective and efficient O&M processes. There was an obvious change in management philosophy from the reliance on school staff to request maintenance (reactive maintenance) to a more proactive maintenance approach. The maintenance program was focused on Preventive Maintenance (PM) and was well documented. There could be enhancements through the incorporation of Predictive Testing and Inspection (PT&I) methods to supplement the PM program. A good understanding of the common problems was evident, as well as a desire for total control

71

of what needs to be done in the school buildings. While there are effective and efficient work management and facility inventory processes, there is an opportunity to improve them thorough documentation of processes.

Implementation of facility audits (facility condition assessments) had been integrated into the overall maintenance and repair program with great success over the past couple years. There were very good project management and construction delivery practices incorporating good communication, project collaboration, and design guidelines. Pre- and post-commissioning is generally conducted, yet there is a stated desire to improve requirements definition and achieve 100% commissioning.

Energy management and sustainability policies were in place and program implementation was beginning to make substantial advancements. Building automation systems were in place in a majority of the schools and portable units took advantage of sensors to improve energy efficiency. Sustainability practices were being incorporated into new school construction and renovations. Initiatives and accomplishments included schools achieving certification as a Green School, comprehensive efforts to reduce energy usage, recycling programs, green cleaning, and Integrated Pest Management (IPM).

Grounds and custodial services operated with a high degree of proficiency to provide safe athletic fields and clean schools with a focus on cleaning for health, not just appearance. Security, life safety, and environmental health and safety programs and awareness of codes, laws, and regulations were among some of the best reviewed in a public school system setting.

Measurement, Analysis, and Knowledge Management: Facility Management technology to support automated work processes and measure performance is accomplished through a legacy system. There should be a strategic plan in place to consider the long-term future of the legacy system and improve the ability to provide credible performance measures for the FM organization. There is a well-defined and well-communicated level of service and recognition of processes to measure performance. There has also been some attempt to benchmark performance. However, this may be the area of greatest potential improvement. Through the evaluation, we identified a number of significant accomplishments and great strides at process improvement, yet limited abilities based on lack of suitable KPIs, for the leadership of the FM organization to demonstrate these accomplishments and prove the value of the facilities organization. The implementation of lean process improvements that have already shown value could be enhanced through more effective performance measurement.

Performance Results: The FM organization appeared to be adequately staffed and takes full advantage of prioritizing funding to create a safe and nurturing school environment to help achieve the mission of the school system. There was documentation regarding performance of the FM organization with respect to customer satisfaction, energy consumption, custodial overtime, and workers compensation incident rates and claims. However, limited documentation of key performance indicators (KPI) relevant to the performance and health of the facilities organization were available.

Accomplishments

Accomplishment #1 – Created a well-structured FM organization suited to achieve the goals of the facilities division and the school system and established a high level of trust among school staff through effective, consistent and proactive communication.

Accomplishment #2 – Implemented a Lean Six Sigma quality improvement program to evaluate and improve FP&M

processes with clear and documented early successes in cost avoidance and budget improvement.

Accomplishment #3 – Leadership involvement in the recruiting process assisted in identifying and attracting talent to the organization.

Accomplishment #4 – Executed a facility condition assessment program to develop a capital asset management plan for the schools in order to enhance the prioritization and budgeting of school maintenance and repairs.

Accomplishment #5 – Implemented effective cost and schedule controls for capital construction projects though the use of design directives, uniform educational specifications and excellent construction project management practices.

Accomplishment #6 – Implemented a comprehensive and successful energy management program and initiated sustainability practices.

Accomplishment #7 – Developed a cost-effective and proactive maintenance program aligned with the mission of the school system.

Accomplishment #8 – Implemented effective health and safety controls for schools through threat and vulnerability analysis, emergency preparedness plans, emergency drills and training, and maintenance of required EH&S plans.

Accomplishment #9 – Implemented process improvements and summer re-scheduling to reduce custodial staff overtime without a reduction in service levels. In 2009, the OT hours were reduced by 50% resulting in savings of over $500,000 in labor costs [verify from $1.1M].

Recommendations

Recommendation 1: Formalize and document facilities planning and maintenance policies and procedures and increase access to the documentation. We recommend creating easier access to important FM services and support by publishing key information and incorporating FM policies and processes. This could include the consolidation of existing polices with needed enhancements in an overall O&M Manual which should include, but not necessarily be limited to the following:

- FM structure and strategy
- Service levels, policies, and safety procedures
- School design and performance guidelines
- Operations and maintenance processes
- Facilities documentation exchange and control
- Facilities management information standards
- Facilities performance measurement (key performance indicators)

Recommendation 2: Development of a facilities balanced scorecard and specific KPIs aligned with the PSS mission. Significant accomplishments and great strides in process improvement were evident in the FM organization. However, there is a need to improve the measurement of performance to tell the successful story of the facilities organization. We recommend implementation of a balanced scorecard of KPIs in alignment with the school system and FM missions to enhance the visibility and position of the facilities organization and continue the strategic focus on the right areas of continuous improvement.

Recommendation 3: Initiate a comprehensive low-cost internal training program with support by more formal external training. We recommend a training program focused on

O&M concepts/philosophy, operational processes, and supporting tools and technology to increase operational alignment and performance. We also recommend enhancing individual training and professional development plans in alignment with the balanced scorecard to minimize possible on-the-job-accidents, staff inefficiencies, repeat work, and ensure that maintenance personnel are knowledgeable in current O&M procedures and techniques.

Recommendation 4: We recommend continued enhancement and support of the energy management/conservation plan and sustainability (green initiatives) policies. There are great sustainability initiatives beginning to be implemented within the FM organization and the school system. However, our experience has shown recent indications of plans failing to deliver on expectations and promises. We recommend focus on some key areas and implementing controls and measures to document the success of the initiatives.

Recommendation 5: Enhance the existing preventive maintenance program with a comprehensive planned maintenance program including streamlined RCM philosophy. We recommend the incorporation of a streamlined Reliability-Centered Maintenance (RCM) philosophy by the incorporation of additional Predictive Testing and Inspection (PT&I) methods and root-cause analyses to supplement the PM program. This will help extend the service life of school facilities, building systems and equipment, as well as maximize the reliability and safety of building systems.

Recommendation 6: Develop a long-term Facility Management information technology plan. The current legacy Computerized Maintenance Management System (CMMS) is well-used and supported; however, it has limited capabilities compared to new Integrated Work Management System (IWMS) and has a greater risk of obsolescence than commercially-available and vendor-supported systems. To minimize risk and allow eventual successful transition to a more enterprise system, we recommend developing a strategic technology plan. Elements of the plan put in place early could also maximize the value of the current system.

The review team's knowledge and experience as successful practitioners of educational facilities management and administration form the judgment and recommendations of this report. That knowledge and experience was combined with an extensive interview process, detailed document review, and studied comparisons. The judgments and recommendations included in this report are given not by way of criticism, but rather as a means to assist the FM division in its effort to continuously improve current levels of service and to better meet the needs of the school system.

Chapter 6: Sample Recommendations

The following sections present examples of practices and knowledge requirements to climb to higher levels in the organizational capability maturity model. They include best practices and important elements that can help the FM reach the summit.

The Business Case for RCM

One of the toughest challenges most facilities departments face is effectively executing a proactive (planned) maintenance program to support the organization's mission with limited funds and staff. Today's climate of focused operational cost cutting makes this even more difficult. We have to respond to emergencies and customer service requests, which leaves precious few areas to reduce labor requirements. Facility Managers often feel helpless investing in and implementing successful planned maintenance programs. Help is here! This challenge may actually present FM departments with one of the best opportunities to enhance efficiency through the use of proven technologies.

Today, some of the best facilities organizations are turning to improved predictive testing technologies and processes to overcome this challenge. The implementation of a streamlined

Reliability-Centered Maintenance (RCM) philosophy by the inclusion of Predictive Testing and Inspection (PT&I) methods can effectively supplement a standard Preventive Maintenance (PM) program and reduce costs at the same time. PT&I methods use specific technologies (such as ultrasonic probes, vibration screening tools, laser alignment tools, and infrared cameras) to gather empirical data on equipment performance to identify when and what preventive maintenance should be done. These technologies and methods can be integrated into the existing PM program at a relatively low cost and level of effort to optimize the program and maximize the reliability of critical systems. In some cases we have seen a reduction in PM levels of effort by 15 to 20 percent by eliminating unnecessary calendar-based tasks or reducing PM frequencies based on empirical condition data.

With few exceptions, preventive maintenance has been considered the most effective way of maintaining building systems and extending the service life of equipment. Most PM programs are based on the assumption that there is a cause and effect relationship between scheduled maintenance and system reliability. The primary assumption is that mechanical parts wear out, thus the reliability of the equipment must be in direct proportion to its operating age. Research has indicated that operating age sometimes may have little or no effect on failure rates. There are many different equipment failure modes, only a small number of which are actually age or use-related. Reliability Centered Maintenance (RCM) was developed to include the optimal mix of reactive-, time- or interval-based, and condition-based maintenance.

RCM is a maintenance philosophy that identifies actions that will reduce the probability of unanticipated equipment failure that are the most cost-effective. The principle is that the most critical facilities assets receive maintenance first, based on their criticality to the mission of the facility or organization dependent on that asset.

Maintainable facilities assets that are not critical to the mission are placed in a deferred or "run to failure" maintenance category, and repaired or replaced only when time permits or after problems are discovered or actual failure occurs.

A streamlined RCM maintenance philosophy allows organizations to use their scarce personnel and funding resources to maintain the most critical assets that have the highest probability of failure and impact to the organization's mission. Streamlined RCM programs have several clear benefits:

1. Managers, not equipment, plan shop technicians' activities and time.
2. Efficiencies are gained by performing maintenance on equipment when needed, not based on the calendar *[The right maintenance on the right equipment at the right time]*.
3. Planning of work allows labor, parts, materials and tools to be available when needed.
4. Equipment part replacements and materials are minimized. The probability that bearings need only lubrication and not replacement is maximized. PM/PT&I also minimizes the potential need to not only replace bearings, but the shaft, rotating parts, bearing housings, casings, and possibly motors.
5. Managers/schedulers have time to evaluate what other work could be done at the same time and location as the planned PM/PT&I, optimizing shop productivity.
6. Engineers can study equipment performance and maintenance histories to conduct root cause analyses or implement changes that could improve equipment performance or energy efficiency.

World class facilities organizations make extensive use of PT&I technologies to gather and analyze data in order to optimize proactive maintenance. The best use of PT&I is to implement simple visual/audible and non-destructive procedures to record conditions at a specific time (snap shot) when the equipment is inspected at the time of PM. When a series of condition records (snap shots) are compiled a trend analysis can be developed. This trend analysis is the basis of PT&I and can also provide factual data to support capital expenditure decisions regarding building systems. Specific PT&I methods that have proven to be effective include:

- Airborne/structure-borne Ultrasonic Testing
- Infrared Thermography (IRT)
- Motor Circuit Analysis (MCA) Testing
- Vibration Screening and Analyses (Rotating Equip.)
- Lubrication Oil Analyses
- Laser Sheave and Shaft Alignment
- Water Chemistry Analysis

The implementation of RCM is a complex endeavor that requires several elements to come together to work effectively. The recommended overall process for integrating RCM processes into facilities O&M is summarized as follows:

1. Identify Systems and Equipment to Maintain
2. Determine Criticality and Performance
3. Evaluate Probability of Failure
4. Determine Failure Modes and Effects
5. Develop Best Maintenance Plans
6. Implement Maintenance
7. Measure Performance and Optimize Program

Reductions in maintenance staff, increased O&M responsibilities, restricted resources, increasing complexity of building systems, and advances in diagnostic tools and technologies have converged to bring RCM to the front and center of facility maintenance best practices. The RCM approach is not just for large and complex manufacturing or production facilities. It has become more mainstream, and continues to grow in popularity in more traditional facilities across a spectrum of industry types. Optimizing the effectiveness and efficiency of the facilities organization and proving a positive return-on-investment of maintenance resources will continue to increase the adoption of RCM processes.

Successes have been shown and well documented by a number of forward-thinking FM organizations. Early adopters of RCM have included government agencies such as NASA, the Department of State, and branches of the Department of Defense. Continued development has been spurred by the Smithsonian Institution's mission to protect the Nation's most treasured artifacts. The growth of RCM has now entered healthcare facilities, corporate facilities (stimulated by the need to better maintain building systems serving critical data centers), and educational institutions in both higher education and even simplified (streamlined) approaches in K-12 public schools.

Publications and increased frequency of journal articles regarding RCM in facilities have also made it easier to understand and implement streamlined RCM processes. Acknowledgement must be given to John Moubray's work regarding RCM captured in his book *Reliability-Centered Maintenance (RCM II"*. Much of the content of this report is based on definitions and concepts presented in his book (Moubray, 2007). In addition, content has been drawn from the National Aeronautics and Space Administration (NASA) Reliability-Centered Maintenance (RCM) Handbook, as well as experience with the Smithsonian's and other RCM programs.

In its purest form, RCM is about optimizing maintenance. The primary focus of RCM is on maximizing the reliability of building systems with cost-effective and efficient processes in performing maintenance. There are both short-term considerations and long-term cost saving implications. In our experience, the added costs of talented maintenance staff and tools to implement the RCM program are more than offset by the short-term efficiencies and long-term life extension of building systems. A summary of some of the benefits of RCM are listed as follows:

- Increased equipment uptime / reliability
- Greater safety and environmental integrity
- Improved operating performance
- Improved energy performance
- Cost-effective maintenance
- Extended useful life of assets
- Comprehensive maintenance database
- Improved motivation
- Better teamwork and scheduling

As a simple example, consider the situation of an air-handling unit failing. The cost of the actual maintenance and repair is fairly low compared to the costs associated with disruption of productivity in the areas being served by the unit. In the case of the Smithsonian's charter, a similar situation may result in damage to artifacts in exhibit areas served by the air-handler due to increased humidity and/or temperature outside the performance standard. Due to the limitations on facilities staffing levels, this condition is all too common. Data and benchmarks show that facilities organizations continue to be too reactive in nature.

The key for any facilities organization is to find the optimal level of maintenance to provide the desired level of service with the available resources at hand. This includes maximizing the return-on-investment for contracted maintenance services. While many organizations strive to be more proactive, it is often done by diving in full force without regard to the cost of implementing comprehensive PM programs. There are even some valuable industry publications that have published tables indicating metric targets of 100 percent PM to achieve a level of service of showpiece facilities[4]. Consider the following figure.

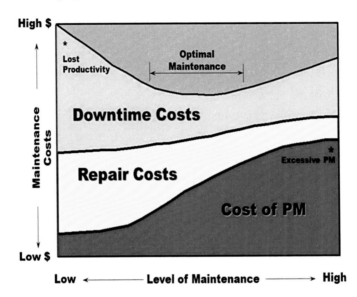

Figure 8: Graphical Representation of RCM

Many facilities organizations still struggle with a majority of their work being reactive. It is not uncommon to find O&M organizations showing work order data that indicates PM to Corrective Maintenance (CM) ratios in the 10 to 20 percent range. This condition is representative of the left-hand side of Figure 8, where the cost of PM labor is low and the costs of reactive labor and repair costs are relatively high. In addition, the downtime costs associated with lost productivity and loss of maintenance productivity are at the highest levels. The result is that the overall

[4] APPA (2002). *Maintenance Staffing Guidelines for Educational Facilities.* APPA. Alexandria, VA.

maintenance and repair costs (including loss of equipment life and value) are highest.

At the other end of the spectrum, to the right-hand side of Figure 1, there are substantial PM costs. It requires skilled, trained, and enough competent staff to maintain equipment at a comprehensive level. In fact, there is a point of diminishing returns. We have had experience with some facilities organizations that have taken it too far in their effort to establish best practice maintenance programs. Excessive PM costs money and can introduce inefficiencies and even equipment failures. While good PM programs do minimize repair costs, there are still associated downtime costs to pull equipment and systems offline to accomplish traditional PM procedures.

The goal is to find the *'sweet-spot'* where reliability of the plant equipment and building systems are maximized at the lowest overall cost of maintenance. To accomplish this requires the introduction of experience-based maintenance practices and predictive testing and inspection techniques. The optimal maintenance zone shown in the chart also considers run-to-failure approaches for non-critical and less expensive assets that may cost more to maintain than replace should they fail. Consider the example of small fractional horsepower in-line circulation pumps that are in non-critical systems. The long-term costs of performing standard scheduled maintenance will most likely exceed the cost to replace the pump should it fail. This practice is typically referred to as *"run-to-failure"*.

This optimization helps to minimize maintenance cost while also minimizing the potential and/or reality of equipment downtime which carries a significantly higher cost potential. Consider the cost for the Smithsonian Institution to replace or restore an artifact damaged by equipment failure. Best-in-class maintenance processes can be determined by an "optimal maintenance" analysis as part of a RCM program.

A Word (or Two) about FM Technology

While this is a book focused on the people component of FM; where FM is defined as a profession that encompasses multiple disciplines to ensure functionality of the built environment by integrating people, place, process and technology[5], we feel the need to address the future impact of technology. People will debate the greatest achievements of humankind until the end of time; whether it is culture, arts, philosophy, science, or technology. And while there is no one conclusive or decisive argument, the impact of technology will stand the test of time. In the modern world it is technology that has played the most dramatic role in shaping the future.

This is also true in the narrower view of facilities and Facility Management. Technology will continue to shape our processes and evolve the role of the people who work in facilities organizations. It is critical that managers who desire to create high performance Facility Management organizations embrace the right technologies. These technologies, today, include smart building technologies, CMMS/IWMS, Building Automation Systems (BAS), Predictive Maintenance (PdM), Automated Fault Detection and Diagnostics (AFDD), as well as the supporting processes and standards such as Building Information Modeling (BIM) & Construction Operations Building information exchange (COBie).

BIM is revolutionizing the way we plan, design & construct facilities. The current value of BIM to the A/E/C – Architecture, Engineering, and Construction community is unquestionable. Soon BIM will realize its true vision of benefiting the entire life-cycle of

---

[5] Definition presented by the International Facility Management Association (IFMA).

facilities when broad acceptance and use adds value to the operations component of the built environment life-cycle. It is the operations and renewals component of the facility life-cycle that is the largest in both time and cost and squarely in the domain of the FM. Collecting data once at the point of creation and effectively managing and accessing the data for O&M can and will generate efficiencies, thereby reducing total costs of ownership. Where once we lacked consistent and accurate data to effectively manage facilities, we now often face a quite different challenge – an overwhelming amount of data from multiple systems.

The high performance Facility Management organization will learn how to optimize the exchange of information in multiple data models. Processes and standards, such as COBie, will enable these data exchanges. In turn, we will get more value out of our CMMS/IWMS. The end result is better information to make the best decisions re: facilities and enable enhanced performance measurement. We cannot optimize our processes without effective use of these information technologies, processes, and technology and data standards.

Another area of concern and opportunity is the evolution of advanced and complex building technologies. Smart buildings and integrated intelligent building systems are challenging the best and brightest operating engineers. Direct Digital Controls (DDC) and computer controls in everything from our BAS to HVAC systems and security and life safety systems are dramatically improving building performance and changing the way we operate building systems. Facility Management organizations now require more sophistication in energy management/BAS and building control technicians. These systems will continue to become more technologically advanced. The use of predictive testing and inspection tools and methods help keep us close, but will eventually give way to even more advance AFDD, that are now being manufactured and introduced into modern buildings.

Technologies within buildings and building systems are not alone in changing the course of FM. Information technologies are changing the way many organizations and institutions do business. Consider the changing landscape of the higher education community. Instructional programs are changing with the use of more classroom technologies and distance learning options have increased dramatically. Students expect to be wired 100 percent of the time while on campus. Corporations are also taking advantage of collaborative meeting tools, connecting people in remote locations and enabling more effective telework environment. Workplaces and spaces today and the future will not resemble those we have become accustomed to.

These technologies are now at a tipping point. We are at the verge of transformational changes in the way we O&M facilities.

Importance of Codes and Regulations

Read the mission statement of just about any facilities organization and you will relate to some very common statements and concepts –*"Our mission is to create, operate, and maintain facilities that provide a safe, secure, healthy, and productive environment that enables the mission of the organization/institution".* It is indeed the Facility Manager's job to understand the quality of building systems and ensure policies and practices that achieve these missions. This is very difficult to achieve without a basic understanding, and in many cases deeper organizational understanding, of building codes and regulations

Building codes establ

minimu

construc

established preventive maintenance program, however, it could benefit from the introduction of technologies such as handheld devices, predictive testing and inspection technologies, and other diagnostic tools.

- One of the biggest challenges the O&M organization faces is the coordination and integration of work across trade shops and campus services teams. There appears to be some lack of understanding of how to best coordinate maintenance activities. Better definition of work roles and integration by documenting and streamlining processes could create efficiencies.
- We identified a need for both overall process and technology training to support both current workflow and enhanced processes. Improved commitment and understanding of both how and why work should be accomplished can be established through an internal training program.
- Finally, there should be more focus on the measurement of key performance indicators aligned with the facilities mission to tell the story of the O&M organization. There is currently limited ability to baseline or track improved performance, thought the tools are available.

Details of key findings, accomplishments and recommendations for initiatives to enhance efficiencies are provided in the following sections. The body of the report contains a prioritization of recommendations.

Summary of Recommendations

Based on our evaluation and findings, we grouped our recommendations into four main categories related to: technologies and tools, workflow processes, performance measurement, and

63

requirements" means that construction and renovations meet the criteria of being "practical and adequate for protecting life, safety and welfare of the public". Building codes embrace all aspects of building construction including: fire & life safety issues, structural design, security, mechanical, electrical & plumbing systems, energy conservation and accessibility. They provide safeguards to ensure uniformity in the construction industry. While codes and standards referenced within the codes provide a means to reduce risks to an acceptable level, no code can totally eliminate all potential hazards.

Today, more than ever, building codes and regulations focus not only on construction, renovations, and alterations, but operations and maintenance of facilities as well. In fact, this is the sole purpose of the International Property Maintenance Code. Even with the other model codes, ensuring that building systems are operated, maintained, inspected and tested to ensure continued safe conditions is paramount. Just look to the National Fire Protection Association (NFPA) and American Society of Heating, Refrigerating, and Air-Conditioning Engineers (ASHRAE) to find standard after standard establishing minimum acceptable practices for maintaining building systems and environments.

Building codes throughout the U.S. vary by state and address not only structural requirements but also establish fire, electrical, safety, and health standards, plus standards for access to, from and within facilities by disabled persons. County and local governments also amend and enact building codes—often to set requirements for regional or locally-specific requirements. There are also federal rules, such as those established in the 1970s for Occupational Safety and Health (OSHA Act) and the 1990s upon passage of the Americans with Disabilities Act. Other common building regulations deal with energy conservation and environmental protection.

workforc
recomme

Technolog

1. Esta
   build......gs, rooms)   ....., equipment, PM,
2. Create IWMS Problem and Repair Codes
3. Link Work Orders to Equipment for Histories
4. Implement Predictive Testing & Inspection (PT&I) Technologies
5. Purchase Other Diagnostic Tools (e.g., trending temperature loggers, controls, etc.)
6. Experiment with Handheld Applications (PM group and stockroom)
7. Test Bar Coding of Equipment for PM
8. Consider Building Automation System (BAS) Upgrades
9. Integrate Graphics and O&M Manuals
10. Develop Dashboards for Supervisors (metrics) – Plasma Displays (situation room) – to show metrics
11. Move to COTS (Commercial-Off-The-Shelf) Space Planning Solution to Support O&M
12. Purchase vehicles for Preventive Maintenance (PM) team

Workflow Processes

13. Work on Supervisor Integration
14. Operations Center and Instrumentation Team Integration
15. HVAC Mechanic / PM Tech / Instrumentation Tech Integration
16. Establish Formal Root Cause Analysis Process (resources)
17. Consider Systems Engineer for BAS Analysis
18. Implement Escalation Process – Reduce Work Order (WO) Aging
19. Document Processes - Defining work better to take away ambiguity and excuses
20. Consider Adding Weekend and Third Shift Supervision
21. Expand Stockroom Hours (i.e. 6 am to 4 pm)

All of these rules exist to ensure not only quality construction that will then protect anyone in or near a building, and the value of the property itself, but equal access and improved productivity and health. Anyone involved in operating and maintaining facilities needs to be well aware of these codes, standards, and regulations and have a working knowledge of what they require.

Chapter 7: Advice from FM Experts

O ver these many years, we have had the great fortune of collaborating with industry experts whose backgrounds and expertise have brought both breadth and depth to the FM industry. Our corporate knowledge has greatly benefited through these highly-valued relationships. In developing the content for this body of work, we decided to reach out to these experts and invite them to contribute to this discussion. Their bios are provided below.

Brad Cowley
Brad Cowley has a wide range of Facility Management experience. A graduate of Brigham Young University's Facility and Property Management program, Brad has been involved in the construction and management of a variety of facilities across the U.S. including: retail, warehouse, educational, office, and assembly spaces. He has managed teams of facility professionals with responsibility for hundreds of locations. Brad is the co-founder of two facility related business and has taught Facility Management courses for operations, maintenance, and technology at his alma

mater. He has held leadership roles with IFMA and has been a featured speaker at World Workplace and other events.

Brad has earned several facility related professional designations including: Construction Document Technologist from the Construction Specifications Institute and Certified Facility Manager from the International Facility Management Association. As a Certified Scrum Product Owner, Brad is currently managing the implementation of an enterprise IWMS for a large multinational organization. His most cherished designations are "husband" to his beautiful with Nicole, and "father" to his four incredible daughters.

Daniel F. Geldermann, P.E., CFM

Dan Geldermann is a principal analyst at CALIBRE, a management and technology services company. Dan has more than 30 years of experience that includes directing all aspects of facilities management to include planning, engineering, design, contracts, operations, maintenance, repair, construction, utilities, environmental, transportation, safety, real estate, historic properties and family housing at various locations across the United States, Asia, and Europe. In addition to his consulting experience, his expertise has been developed through a career as a U.S. Navy Civil Engineer Corps officer and as an associate director of facilities at a state university.

Dan is a registered Professional Engineer in Wisconsin and Virginia, a Certified Facility Manager, and holds a Master Facility Executive Certificate from the Building Owners & Management Institute. He is a past Chairman of the Society of American Military Engineers (SAME) National Facilities Management Committee, and was a study member on the National Research Council of the National Academies' 2012 publication *"Predicting Outcomes of Investments in Maintenance and Repair of Federal Facilities"*. He holds a B.S. degree in civil engineering from Marquette University and a M.S. degree in management from the U.S. Naval Postgraduate School.

Kevin Moulton

Kevin is a Senior Business Consultant for PacifiCorp Energy in Salt Lake City, Utah. Kevin earned his Bachelor of Science degree in Facilities & Property Management from Brigham Young University and an MBA from Hawaii Pacific University. He has worked in the facilities management field as a consultant, analyst and FM in several parts of the country. He has specialized in developing operations, maintenance and capital budgets for large corporations and utilizing FM tools to aid executive management teams in effective maintenance and capital investment prioritization.

Kevin Santee

Kevin is a degreed chemist and certified industrial hygienist (CIH). He has spent the past twenty years with the U.S. General Services Administration, the Federal government's primary property manager. Over the course of those years, he has worked in all the business lines associated with facilities management including: operations and maintenance, custodial service, childcare, environmental health and safety, and financial management. Kevin is currently the GSA CMMS regional systems administrator and has been serving on a GSA national CMMS team for the past year.

Mark Sekula, FMP, LEED-AP, CFM, IFMA Fellow

Mark is President of Facility Futures, Inc. a global Facility Management consulting firm in Milwaukee. With over 36 years of Facility Management experience, he has served as a facilities management practitioner and as an FM consultant. He is a certified instructor of the International Facility Management Association (IFMA) and teaches classes in Facility Management nationally. He is also an instructor at Northern Illinois University in the Facility Management Program.

A Certified Facility Manager since 1993, Mark has served on the board of the International Facility Management Association's Southeast Wisconsin Chapter and as a director on the IFMA International Board of Directors. He founded the IFMA Facility Management Consultants Council and has served as an officer of the Southeast Wisconsin IFMA Chapter. In 2011, he was bestowed the highest honor given by the International Facility Management Association (IFMA) when he was named an IFMA Fellow. Mark also co-authored the recently published book titled, *"The Facility Manager's Field Guide"* as well as having had over 25 articles published on Facility Management and business issues in a variety of professional journals.

Mark holds a Bachelor of Science degree in Architectural Studies from the University of Wisconsin-Milwaukee School of Architecture and Urban Planning and a certificate from the Kellogg Management Institute-Management Certificate Program at Northwestern University.

Pieter van der Have, CEFP

Pieter has a wealth of experience in facilities management, particularly in higher education. Pieter is a past president of APPA, Certified Educational Facilities Professional (CEFP) and instructor in APPA's professional credentialing program. He has led a 600-person organization at the University of Utah, progressing literally from the ground floor of the organization to the level of Assistant Vice President for Plant Operations. He retired from the University of Utah on June 30, 2006. Pieter is currently Director of the Facility Management degree program at Weber State University.

His responsibilities at the university extended well beyond routine maintenance and operations of this 10-million gsf campus. He was deeply involved in planning, programming, design, and construction of new facilities, including several renowned research facilities and hospitals. Pieter was the chair of the Olympic Operations Planning Committee for 2002 Winter Olympics hosted by the University of Utah, a group that functioned for nearly six years as planning and coordination with the Salt Lake Olympic Committee (SLOC) progressed.

Steve Vollmer

Steve is the Director of the Office of Facilities Management for Fairfax County Public Schools (FCPS) in Northern Virginia. His office is comprised of 497 employees maintaining 26.9 million square feet of space in 196 buildings. FCPS is the 11th largest public school district in the United States. Steve has served the FCPS' facilities management group for over 29 years and is a Certified Facility Manager (CFM).

Fred Weiss, CFM

Fred is the Facility Management Regional Business Operations Manager for H-E-B. Previously, he held similar positions at The University of Texas at San Antonio, TX and the Research and Engineering Center of Ford Motor Company (Dearborn, MI) managing facilities operating budgets, key performance indicators, business continuity planning teams, strategic facility planning, and many other Facility Management functions.

Fred has more than 25 years of in-depth and diverse facilities experience. The majority of his background has been in the private sector with facilities management organizations responsible for research, engineering, and headquarters facilities.

He is an active member of the International Facility Management Association (IFMA) for more than 25 years. Presently, he serves on the Board of Directors of the San Antonio Chapter of IFMA. He is a member of the Academic Facilities Council of IFMA and is a subject matter expert for several IFMA task forces. He received a BBA from Eastern Michigan University, and MBA from Wayne State University. Fred has attended the FBI Citizens Academy. In October 2005, he was awarded IFMA's highest honor, IFMA Fellow.

Robert Wilkinson

Robert is the Director for Maintenance and Operations at Frederick County Public Schools (FCPS). FCPS is recognized as one of the premier school systems, not just in the state of Maryland, but nationally. The mission of the Facilities Services Division is to "plan and maintain schools and other facilities, with the goal of creating optimal learning environments conducive to safety and success for all students and staff.

FCPS has a total of 63 schools containing approximately 6.5 million square feet of educational space. There are 10 high schools, 13 middle schools, 36 elementary schools, and four other alternative schools and educational buildings. There are also additional support and administrative buildings.

Robert has a B.S. in Aerospace Engineering from Pennsylvania State University, an M.B.A. from Hood College, and is currently pursuing an M.A. in Psychology. Prior to joining FCPS, he worked in defense contracting, public works, and in school maintenance and operations.

Alexander Willman

Alex has a Bachelor of Science in Mechanical Engineering from Lehigh University and a   Master of Science in Architectural

Engineering from Pennsylvania State University. He is a licensed Professional Engineer in the Commonwealth of Virginia. Alex is currently Branch Chief, Maintenance Support Division, Office of Facility Management, Bureau of Overseas Buildings Operations, U.S. Department of State. In this position he is responsible for managing staff charged with the efficient allocation of $76 million in sustainment funding to 270 embassies and consultants. He also directs the production of budget estimates for future building operating expenses at planned New Embassy Compounds and Consulates.

Prior to joining OBO, Alex was the Energy Program Manager for Lockheed Martin Corporation in Rockville, MD. There he managed the development for EPA of the first Energy Star$^{©}$ Label for Buildings website and directed staff and consultants for $9M multi-year contract for the Federal Energy Management Program of the U. S. Department of Energy.

Alex was also Director of Engineering and Indoor Air Programs, National Energy Management Institute, Alexandria VA; where he was responsible for technical due diligence and energy monitoring for nation-wide energy savings performance contracts. Alex is a Lieutenant (j.g.), U. S. Naval Reserve and honored with a Vietnam Service Medal.

———————

To focus the discussion, we identified key issues and developed a set of relevant questions to which we captured their responses. Each question is provided below followed by each contributor's response. By framing it in this manner, we determined that this would enable the reader to obtain the varied expert perspectives that revolve around each issue.

In your view, what are the top two issues within the FM community that are requiring the inordinate attention of owners/managers, possibly causing them unnecessary pain?

Cowley: *"I think what keeps business owners up at night with regard to facilities is how the overall economy and pending regulatory legislation may affect their facility decisions. Because the costs associated with facilities are so high, changes in the economy or legislation can have a significant impact on an organization's financial status. Business owners benefit from having access to facility expertise (in-house or outsourced) as it relates to these two topics."*

van der Have: *"The FM community, at least at the senior level, is an aging community. There are estimates floating around that nearly a third of current senior leadership will retire (or pass away) over the next 5-10 years. That in itself may offer opportunities for new blood and ideas. However, employers are increasingly looking for candidates outside the organization; simply having years of experience within the organization is no longer a guarantee for promotion. On a related note, expectations are that candidates have at least a bachelor's degree in a field related to facilities management. As we look around, it appears that there is currently a void of qualified candidates for future senior leadership positions.*

Buildings and systems are becoming increasingly high tech and sophisticated. Some would say that our newest buildings are smarter than we are. Existing staff across the breadth of the FM organization, many of whom may have been employed in FM for years, have to be continually trained in order to stay up with current and future technologies. For the most part, FM departments have never been able to come up with enough budget dollars to provide adequate training. With the twists and turns in our recent economies, there is a real danger that our technicians are falling further behind technologically, potentially compromising the sustenance of our facilities and other infrastructure."

100

Santee: *"My experience is limited to the Federal Government perspective and specifically the General Services Administration (GSA). From my GSA perspective, the current critical issues are:*

1. *Capturing and using data correctly*
2. *Keeping up with FM advances in technology and work practices*

Facility management in the Government has evolved dramatically from a prescriptive, reactive approach to a focus on performance-based customer service. Along with this, we've experienced a flood of facility and customer data. The data represents the diversity of Federal agency operations and GSA's own complexity of operations. Most of today's data is real-time with a short life, delivered by new technology. Our challenge is prioritizing critical data and making the data actionable while it is still valid. Rapid advances in FM technology have made this more challenging by increasing the quantity and breadth of data available to the GSA facility manager. With new technology and work practices comes the need to educate staff. The education is a challenge due to the sometimes overlapping nature of new and existing technology. Integrating new work practices is also challenging because GSA's customer base consists of all Federal agencies, who have their own unique practices, requirements and limitations."

Vollmer: *"One large area facility managers have had to address increasingly in the past few years is providing exceptional indoor air quality (IAQ) and occupant comfort while balancing those needs with today's emphasis on minimizing our impact on the environment and reducing energy consumption. Today's facility user is very sophisticated and demands an exceptional environment in which to work, learn, shop or visit. Users are increasingly aware of common*

IAQ issues such as mold or poor humidity control. Users also want stable temperatures that meet the needs of the function taking place in the facility. At the same time, there is growing pressure from the public to minimize the environmental impact (carbon footprint) facilities can have, while facility owners and financial managers insist on minimizing energy costs.

To address that, facility managers need to ensure that the mechanical systems in their facilities are properly maintained and adjusted to ensure they are working properly in order to provide maximum comfort, minimum energy consumption, and proper indoor air quality. Older, but still relevant, systems may have to be "re-commissioned" to ensure facility managers are getting the maximum output for their investment. Old and antiquated systems may need to be budgeted for replacement.

Electrical systems, particularly indoor and outdoor lighting, should be surveyed to determine if they are outdated and can be replaced with newer, more energy efficient lighting. Often, replacement can be done if energy savings can pay back the cost of the project within a timeline acceptable to the financial manager. One caveat is to research what is available and pick what is proven and will outlive the initial investment. There are currently many types of new systems becoming available and some of these systems, or the companies that produce them, will not be around several years from now.

Another area of concern is the proliferation of new codes and laws that must be addressed by facility managers. This is particularly true of facility managers with in-house maintenance staff. Examples include Federal and State-mandated activities such as electrical arc flash analysis and labeling of facilities and training of staff exposed to arc flash hazards; EPA requirements regarding landscaping nutrient and other environmental runoff; the 2010 Americans with Disabilities Act; expanding OSHA requirements;

and state and local laws regarding stormwater management. Today's facility manager needs to be kept abreast of these changing requirements so those applicable to his or her facility can be addressed. If necessary, funding can be sought to comply with new laws and regulations. Not doing so can place the facility owner at risk of severe fines and penalties."

Sekula: Issue 1: Attract and Retain – PART 1

  "Lately CEO's have often been asked the question, "What are the most critical issues you and your organization will face in the coming years?" Their answer? Attracting and retaining great employees.

  According to the U.S. Department of Labor Bureau of Labor Statistics, in 2008 there were slightly more than 154 million civilian workers in the United States and close to 28 million of them were 55 years of age or over. By 2018 that number will climb to 40 million. At the same time workers between the ages of 25 and 54 numbered 104 million in 2008 but are expected to grow to only 105 million in 2018.

  The American workforce is changing and companies cannot stay static in how they support their employees. What worked yesterday will not work tomorrow. Attracting and retaining the best and most talented employees will become more difficult in the future. The stable of available employees will be thin and companies will need to pull out all stops to demonstrate they are an employer of choice.

  The next generation of workers, commonly referred to as the Generation Y, or the Millennials, have different needs when it comes to work. They are more attuned to technology to help them get their work done. They will also need different kinds of spaces to perform different kinds of work during the course of the day, such as focused work, collaborative work, learning, and socialization. Most office space plans are still very traditional and do not support this new way of working. Thus supporting these four diverse forms of work will certainly pose challenges to facility managers.

Of course attracting and retaining the best employees goes well beyond providing a well-designed workplace that supports the work and the work attitudes of the new workforce. Things like benefits, corporate social responsibility and culture certainly come into play and in many cases trump the workplace. But as the furniture manufacturer Herman Miller points out, "As a strategic tool, the workplace is a vehicle that enables individuals and groups, supports processes and tools, and reflects the organization and its brand".

The physical workplace may not be the number one attractor for these new workers but at the end of the day with three equal job offers in hand, a physical workplace that allows them to work the way they need to in a corporate culture that allows flexible work schedules just may be the tipping point.

The Millennials are coming and we all need to adapt to their needs. Facility managers will be under increased pressure to provide a new physical workplace that meets the needs of the new generation of worker at a reasonable cost."

Issue 2: Attract and Retain – PART 2

"Just as entire organizations will have to fight to attract and retain the best employees, so will facility managers. Facility management is not a profit center. It is not perceived as a creative, innovative profession. It's just not sexy and until facility managers change that perception they will have problems attracting the best employees to the facility management profession.

Back in the day most FM professionals came from allied professions like architecture and engineering. Many facility

104

managers fell into their jobs by accident. Human Resource professionals and office managers in smaller companies were often tapped to handle facility issues and as the company grew those "side jobs" became their full time job. Now there are degreed programs in facility management. But just because there are new degree programs doesn't mean young people will be attracted to them.

The issue we face as a profession is convincing young students to consider facility management as a profession. We must reach out to students and make them aware of our profession. It is paramount that we talk to students in allied college degree programs like construction and interior design. We must tell them that facility management exists and is a potential and viable career opportunity for them. We must also dig even deeper and talk to high school and middle school students who are just starting to think about their future careers. We have to go into their classrooms and create excitement about our profession.

There isn't a more diverse profession than ours and the myriad of things we deal with every day makes the job interesting, challenging and fulfilling. We must encourage the next generation of workers to consider facility management as a profession. We can have an immediate positive impact upon our fellow employees and help them be successful by planning, designing and managing our workplaces and our buildings in new and innovative ways.

As veteran facility managers we know and understand this. Now we have to tell the next generation of workers."

Wilkinson: *"There is no substitute for trustworthy vendors. It is difficult in the public sector, especially given the mandated competition in procurement, to establish and maintain relationships with vendors. But the value of a trusted vendor is immeasurable when they offer advice and material resources that you need in a*

105

timely manner. Public sector FM departments need to find a way to work cooperatively with their procurement professionals to establish viable access to these vendors.

Personnel management is also challenging in the public sector. We need to work to foster a better understanding of the FM needs and their status in the labor market. It seems like the information technology professionals have enjoyed almost unbridled acceptance over the past twenty years or so. Human Resources has recognized and responded to the IT demands. I do not think that there is commensurate regard for FM professionals. Yet, anyone who has access to a highly-skilled building automation system technician knows that this individual is invaluable to your success. Getting others to recognize and regard the value of individuals like these technicians remains a challenge."

What is the FM community not giving enough attention to that, by continuing to do so, will potentially cause greater challenges downstream?

Cowley: *"Again I would reference legislation. I have noticed that local municipalities have sometimes turned to increased fees as a way of raising revenue. If businesses are not paying attention, or don't have someone to advocate their position, local representatives can effectively change the rules of the game by passing legislation that significantly impacts business in their area. I'm thinking of a situation I heard about recently where a city hired a consultant to help them with decreasing tax revenues, due to the down economy. The consultant convinced the city to change the way they calculated storm water charges. The changes that were implemented had significant cost implications for local businesses. The FM industry is good at reacting to changing legislation, but I don't know that the FM industry is involved enough* *with influencing legislation that may affect their organization before it passes."*

van der Have: *"There are widely held beliefs that higher education, as we know it today, is in trouble. Some pundits believe that nearly half of the institutions (including public ones) might fall into bankruptcy in the next fifty years. To a lesser extent, the same might be true for other types of organizations. K-12 buildings tend to be old and archaic, requiring huge amounts of cash inflow to upgrade or replace; or, the buildings are brand-new and sophisticated, often not receiving adequate attention to assure the expected longevity of the buildings and their systems. Health care is going through a metamorphosis as politicians and the public struggle with the cost of providing health care. The federal government is going through a significant budget adjustment which is certain to have an impact on the nature of facilities management.*

All the above situations demand that the FM community has to be nimble and flexible—a characteristic that has not commonly been identified among FM leadership. We have said for years that we need to adapt to change—better yet, anticipate and steer change. The only slightly rhetorical question is: are we ready to do that?"

Santee: *"I would have to say reliability centered maintenance (RCM). The concept and means to implement RCM methods has existed for years. However, manufacturers, installers and maintenance staff continue to focus almost exclusively on preventive maintenance methods. RCM has been proven to reduce maintenance costs, is relatively straight-forward thanks to advances in field analytical equipment and is not difficult to comprehend. Failing to push RCM will continue to result in catastrophic asset failures, in my opinion. Technology advances like BIM and Smart* *buildings will be sorely underutilized if their output is not used to manage assets in a predictive or comprehensive manner.*

Weiss: *Lower the total cost of facility operations. For many organizations, one of the largest numbers/assets on their balance sheet is the facility. And the way you manage the facility can help you keep the cost of ownership as low as possible on the expense side of the income statement. Lower operating costs come in many forms. It begins with the ability to identify all facility operating costs. It includes but is not limited to energy efficiency programs, eliminating non-value added facility services, smaller footprint office sizes, standardization of office accommodations".*

If you had the audience of newly emerging FM professionals in front of you and had only a short time to leave them with an important message about how to be effective as an FM professional, what would your message be?

Cowley: *"My honest answer to that question is to tell them to first get a good technical understanding of building systems and construction methods, and to combine that with a solid understanding of how real estate, business, and particularly the business they will be supporting, work. I would emphasize that they learn the language of finance, and how to frame business decisions and recommendations in a way that will be easily understood by senior management. Finally, I would encourage them to connect with senior professionals in the industry to listen and learn from their wisdom which comes from experience. This will save them a lot of time trying to reinvent the wheel. This networking may also include joining professional associations and seeking out updates to new laws and regulations through news feeds, or specific websites".*

van der Have: *"Aside from the points raised above, FM professionals must learn to communicate, to the fullest meaning of the word. We have not always excelled at this skill.*

They must learn how to present, how to truly listen, how to write effectively. They must be comfortable communicating with individuals from all walks of life, at all levels of the organization. As they guide the organization through the maze of changes that are unavoidable, they must be able and willing to communicate with all types of stakeholders, collecting feedback as well as providing it. They must be able to communicate at the level of their audience, avoiding the use of FM jargon when in an audience with non-FM individuals.

They must be seen as honest, fair, and proactive, and not as an inflexible nay-sayer."

Geldermann: *"Regardless of the levels of facility management knowledge and technical competence that each new FMs brings to the field, there are several areas that all FMs can address to increase their effectiveness and chances for success: be proactive and communicate and interact with people; make a physical connection with your facilities; and think ahead. Hopefully this will enable you to reach a final piece of advice - have fun.*

Be proactive and communicate and interact with people – You are responsible for the safety of people through the upkeep and performance of inanimate objects and machinery. You will be successful managing facilities if you positively communicate and interact with people. You cannot manage facilities from a desk or from off-site as well as you can if you are routinely present and approachable. BAS systems are great, but automation tends to make a maintenance organization more invisible than they intend to be, and this allows customers to not notice or forget about the support they are receiving. Remember that your occupants are your customers and the reason you have a job; and your maintenance team will be the reason for your success - stay approachable and humble.

Meet both customers and maintenance staff as soon as possible and let them know you are available to address their facility concerns and problems. Let customers see you in their spaces, but do not monopolize a customer's time or interfere with their daily activities. Pay attention to communicating with everyone. Notices of planned building service interruptions should be distributed several times before an event, and by several methods (e.g. emails, posters, newsletters, etc.).

When unplanned outages occur, provide an estimated outage restoration time as quickly as possible, and later explain the cause and actions taken to correct the situation and prevent a recurrence. If you say you will follow-up on a request- do it! Both your credibility and your maintenance organization are on the line every time a request is received. Do not immediately say "no" to a customer request, even if you suspect that is the correct answer. Sincerely look into the request and if you or the organization cannot fulfill it, let the customer know the reason for that decision in a timely manner. This could be anything such as "can you paint an office out of cycle", "provide extra custodial service", or "keep the heat on Saturday"? When a request is turned down, offer an alternative action or solution if possible.

Make a physical connection with your facilities - You need to confirm that your buildings are safe, functioning properly, and meeting the comfort, cleanliness and support needs of your customers. Conduct an initial walk-through with your senior maintenance staff member shortly after starting your job and document conditions with photos and notes. Afterwards regularly walk your facilities and become familiar with their layout and

110

condition. Vary the day and times of these visits so you can observe the operations and staff activities at different times of the day and under varying operating conditions. Look for changes from your last visit because variations can indicate improvements or developing problems. Also make occasional afterhours and weekend visits to confirm building automation system energy set-backs are working as programmed, and that the maintenance and custodial staffs are operating safely and productively. Enter every space you can and visit the roof. Restroom and mechanical space cleanliness are good indicators to assess the health and condition of a facility. Their conditions will give you an immediate feel for the level of workforce pride at a facility.

Clean and stocked restrooms, a roof without loose debris or sharp objects, and clean mechanical spaces indicate attention to detail and pride of workmanship or ownership. Clean equipment also makes it easier to spot new leaks or problems. Just wiping down equipment provides a maintenance staff member an opportunity to review control locations and shut-offs, and to recognize changes from the last visit and address developing problems before they escalate. Make sure you continually recognize and compliment the efforts and professionalism shown by the maintenance staff at a well-kept facility.

However, if your initial walk-through reveals unsafe conditions, un-stocked and dirty or smelly restrooms, roofs with trash and loose objects, mechanical spaces and nooks and crannies that are being used as unorganized storage spaces, or as unintended break rooms that are filled with dust, cobwebs, magazines with censored content, newspapers and old chairs, you can probably conclude that your organization is subsidizing naps during working hours and not running as effectively as possible. Tell your senior maintenance staff member to have safety issues corrected and the spaces cleaned-up before your next visit, and to spread the word that mechanical rooms and out of the way spaces are no longer to be used for excess breaks. Do not make it a blame game the first time; just explain that as a team we are going forward to implement changes that will continually improve the facilities. If resources are needed, develop a plan to address problems with team participation to obtain buy-in. Varying the times of your future visits also discourages the use of mechanical spaces for unapproved breaks. If you are too junior to be in charge of staff, invite your boss along on your next visit and share your discoveries. Hopefully the boss has just been too busy, rather than indifferent, and has hired you for help. There is a saying to remember, "You get what you inspect," if the boss is paying attention, so will the staff members.

Think ahead – There are recurring events and common emergencies each year that seem to be a surprise to some maintenance organizations. To them regular seasonal grounds maintenance efforts such as snow clearing and spring landscaping, or equipment changeovers from heating to air conditioning, are treated as unexpected last minute events. The same surprise and inaction can be exhibited when a chiller or boiler unexpectedly breaks down. In addition to routine equipment shut-downs and start-ups, just as important to customers are annual recurring building events or activities that require FM support. These events can be anticipated and planned for to avoid last minute reactive efforts.

FMs should review preventive maintenance schedules and ask questions to learn if equipment is being properly serviced while operating, and during its off season to be ready for smooth start-ups when needed. For customer events, look though any available past organizational materials or newsletters to identify recurring annual events. Request access to and become familiar with emergency service procedures and service support arrangements in the event of fires, major storms, mechanical breakdowns, utility outages, or water system breakages. Are emergency and staff recall phone numbers updated and available? Does your organization documents and know where water shut-off valves are when needed; or will the one maintenance person who knows all that information by memory be on vacation the day your water main breaks? (That was a bad day.)

Lastly, have fun. Facility management done well should bring you a feeling of contributing to your organization's success and a sense of accomplishment. Managing buildings is like having really cool toys to play with that are way too big to bring home."

Moulton: *"One of the great challenges facing facility managers today is prioritizing ever-growing demands with ever-shrinking budgets. The "Great Recession" has taken its toll on the FM's ability to meet 100% of his stakeholder's expectations. As resources become scarce, the FM is frequently faced with the challenge of doing those things with short-term benefit while creating long-term issues.*

The prioritization of maintenance, capital improvements, etc., are often made based on limited information and stakeholder 'wants' with little regard for the future consequences of those decisions. Often, the rationale for making these short-sighted decisions is that eventually the recession will subside, money will begin to flow more freely, budgets will improve and the FM can begin to address the growing backlog of important maintenance that he has neglected in the short-term. The problem with this mindset is that the facilities are typically viewed by management as a cost center. Budgets will be allocated to areas of an organization that provide the greatest benefit for the money and facilities are frequently overlooked in this regard. The backlog of maintenance and capital

113

improvements will continue to build and the problems will become worse.

Effective FM's have the ability to utilize evaluation and improvement tools to both demonstrate and communicate the long-term future impact of maintenance and capital investment decisions. A simple cost/benefit analysis can go a long way in helping stakeholders to understand the importance and long-term implications of difficult decisions facing an FM. FM's who are able to develop a logical approach and methodology in providing concise and useful information to his stakeholders will find that resources will be made available to address the needs of his facilities".

Santee: *"Since an FM professional covers a wide berth, I will choose to limit my audience to those who are responsible for daily operations and maintenance of a facility. To them I would emphasize technology. Do whatever you can to become proficient in the IT technology of your field. The difference makers are those whose systems are like second nature to them. The "geeks" of FM who use email, spreadsheets, virtual conferencing, databases and related building IT apps on stationary and mobile devices will succeed more than others. FM is a relationship and asset management business. The asset and data-centric component has grown exponentially in the last two decades. Learn to type fast, play video games, attend software classes; whatever it takes to make you more comfortable with the data and technology will make your job easier".*

Vollmer: *"New facility managers must first, and foremost, be effective communicators. The new facility manager must present a professional, effective image at all times and proper communication is paramount. Emails, memos, proposals, and other written communication should always be professional, collaborative, grammatically correct, and persuasive. Verbal communication*

114

should be professional and collegial. Poor verbal or written communication portrays an image of unprofessionalism and the FM professional who communicates poorly is not viewed as being on the same level as other departments within the organization. FM professionals should also seek out important decision makers to build relationships that will provide opportunities to illustrate that the FM group are key players in the organization's success. It will also provide "face time" to ask for support, either financially or operationally, for critically needed projects.

Operationally, new facility managers need to quickly establish a system to identify, document, and preventively maintain the buildings and systems for which they are responsible. Many FM professionals don't quantify exactly what equipment and systems are in their buildings. This often leads to reactive rather than preventive maintenance, which typically results in premature and sometimes catastrophic failures, service disruption to facility occupants, loss of work time by facility occupants, and an increased cost to get major systems repaired or replaced on an emergency basis. Documenting facility assets also permits cost forecasting of the replacement of equipment and systems based on life-cycle or condition assessment".

Weiss: *"Many Facility Managers (FMs) are responsible for managing a facility that has been planned by someone (typically an architect) and provided by another (usually built by a contractor). In my past experience, as an FM I was seldom asked to participate in any planning phases for providing the place where people work.*

Get involved as quickly as possible in the planning processes. If you will be managing the maintenance process (whether in-house staff or contracted services), ensure the housekeeping/janitorial closets are large enough to store sufficient supply of daily restroom products; is there a drain line for new high velocity air hand dryers; have staff been trained on new building automation systems; is your budget sufficient for staff and maintenance supplies; does the maintenance staff have the latest as-built drawings; if the as-builts are electronic files do you have a computer system available to the staff 24x7 that is capable of reading the files.

Does the FM department have a business continuity plan unique to its own department? The FM staff is very good at taking care of their customers. However, if a work stopping emergency occurs, the FM department needs to help themselves before they can help others. It's just like the flight attendant says – if the oxygen drops from the ceiling, put it on yourself first, then assist the person next to you."

Wilkinson: *"I am enamored with the quote: "For every complex question, there is a simple answer-- and it's wrong". (Note: I will decline to provide an attribution for this quote for fear that people's opinion of the author will cloud the significance of the quote.) It is never easy to explain a difficult situation to those that lack training and experience in your field. You will never succeed in convincing everyone of the complexity of your tasks. I intentionally work at avoiding overanalyzing every situation (i.e., the proverbial "analysis paralysis"), but it is difficult when we are trained to approach tasks in a deliberate fashion, and when we seek to deliver exceptional and error-free performance.*

You must choose when it's prudent to take a simple approach to resolve a problem. You are not always afforded the time to fully analyze your options, and even when you have the time, you may be poorly-perceived for wasting time on what appears to be a simple issue. I recently read that the U.S. Marines train their officers to be decisive under stress by embracing the "70% solution". The concept is that, despite lacking all of the pertinent information, a timely decision that can be adjusted or corrected is preferable to no decision at all. The author further indicates that mistakes are tolerated if they are not repeated and if they lead the decision-maker to subsequent, improved performance. In the end, you can develop decisiveness, and you will need this trait for the many emergency situations that you encounter. This leads me to my last bit of wisdom. A trusted coworker once told me that "in an emergency, the first information reports are always wrong". He has proven to be correct more often than not. So, the 70% solution that can later be adjusted is a prudent tactic. In fact, you may be exercising the 70% solution in emergencies whether you know it or not."

Willman: *"My message would be: "Learn all you can about the financial drivers for your organization". The training and education that you have to become an FM professional should be the basis for you to "talk the talk" with engineers, technicians, and contractors to effectively operate and maintain facilities. They will tell you costs and savings of new or updating equipment and systems. For you to be recognized as a member of the organization's management team, it is essential to translate the technology solutions needed to optimize operations, into ROI, NPV, and IRR – or whatever financial term is your organization's financial KPI."*

Given the changing landscape within FM which includes new laws, regulations, and mandates pertaining to a broad spectrum of FM related issues (sustainability, technology, workforce development), what should the FM industry be doing to be better prepared and equipped to address these areas?

Cowley: *"I'd love to see a centralized, authoritative source that gathers updates about all these topics and provides them to the* *industry is a simplified form. What is the change, how does it affect you, and what are the best practices surrounding that changes? Right now it seems like that information comes from a variety of sources and it's sometimes difficult to know what the real impact will be. When I hear about changing regulations from vendors, I often assume they are sharing the information in an effort to sell me product or services related to the change. When I look into it deeper I sometimes learn that they presented worst case scenarios about the impact the changes will have, and learn that I have several options to address the changes in my business. An authoritative, unbiased source for these changes would be valuable to me."*

van der Have: *"FM professionals should do more to prepare themselves to be successful business leaders. At the senior level, they are running a business with many diverse activities and responsibilities. Simply to be technically competent in one or two areas is not enough. Simply to have been successful elsewhere in the organization will not suffice. They must learn to guide, to lead, and provide vision and purpose. To be successful at this, leaders should jump at every opportunity to develop these skills in themselves as well as in members of the executive leadership team. They must become willing to take risks, think outside the traditional limits of acceptable FM paradigms, and explore new opportunities. Undoubtedly, this will require an understanding of financial principles, building a business model, calculating ROIs and life cycle costing. We are not merely in the business of operating and maintaining buildings. We are the stewards of expensive assets, while providing a safe haven for all the people, programs and activities that are entitled to exist in our organizations".*

Santee: *"I believe the profession should focus on those issues that are most impactful and have the greatest probability of success. At*

GSA, funding is a primary concern; so issues and initiatives like new technology or education requirements may receive a lower priority due to insufficient funding. Like most industries, issues with the broadest impact that have clear potential for cost savings have a greater chance for success and therefore receive higher priority."

Willman: *"While recognizing that the FM professional has advanced tremendously in the past twenty years, there is an ever increasing pace of change in the management of the built environment. One example is the increasing acceptance of cloud computing that will continue the rapid downsizing of corporate server farms, and the resulting decline of large-scale IT hardware. This and other IT-driven changes to the practice of traditional facilities management means that FMs need to re-define their corporate roles. A change of title is needed to "infrastructure asset managers". Wikipedia defines this as:*

> *Infrastructure asset management is the combination of management, financial, economic, engineering, and other practices applied to physical assets with the objective of providing the required level of service in the most cost-effective manner. It includes the management of the whole life cycle (design, construction, commissioning, operating, maintaining, repairing, modifying, replacing and decommissioning/disposal) of physical and infrastructure assets.[6] Operating and sustainment of assets in a constrained budget environment require some sort of prioritization scheme.*

---

[6] http://en.wikipedia.org/wiki/Asset_management#cite_note-I

This concept has been identified in U.S. transportation planning and management: Asset management is a systematic process of operating, maintaining, upgrading, and disposing of assets cost-effectively, (American Association of State Highway and Transportation Officials). Thus, experienced FMs need to prepare mentally and educationally to acquire the financial skills needed to become Infrastructure Asset Managers. In the typical corporate structure, this position would report directly to the CFO. Technical training must be coupled with the appropriate levels of finance and accounting training, in order for FMs to "talk the talk" of the CFO, in their new role as the Infrastructure Asset Manager."

Chapter 8: A Call to Action

Facility manager's roles and responsibilities are as diverse as the myriad of facilities they manage. Creating, operating, and maintaining high performance corporate, government, educational, healthcare, and R&D facilities require broad individual skills. FM organizations may also number in the thousands or be represented by that lone ranger necessitating the wearing of multiple hats and relying on savvy contracting skills. As a Facility Manager, we understand all too well the complexity and breadth of the core competencies required to successfully enable the mission of our parent organizations. It is not just individual skills that we must focus on, but we must develop sound FM organizational capabilities acting in and aligned and integrated fashion.

IFMA has created effective mechanisms to evaluate a Facility Manager's skills through our education and professional credentials. IFMA's Facility Management Professional (FMP), Certified Facility Manager (CFM), and Sustainability Facility Professional (SFP) credentials are recognized as industry standards for verification of FM core competencies. These credentials are based on Global Job Task Analyses (GJTA) that cover 11 core competencies and hundreds of performance areas. While they assess a FM's individual skills across the broad array of responsibilities, it is the rare FM that covers all aspects of these competencies on a weekly, monthly or even yearly basis. More importantly is the ability

121

of the credentialed Facility Manager to understand the requirements, align the skills with the mission, and integrate individual skills of the organization (or service providers) to accomplish the job.

It is not just individual skills that are important to the Facility Manager, but finding and organizing these skills into organizational capabilities. The goal of a Facility Manager is to provide a work environment an organization needs to achieve its mission. This is best done by integrating people, places, processes, and technologies to optimize the value of facilities throughout their life cycle—that is, from planning, design, and construction through operations and maintenance, renewal, and ultimately disposal.

High performance Facility Management requires the knowledge, skills and abilities to deliver services at a high level, and the physical infrastructure to deliver those services in an economical, environmentally friendly, and people-friendly workplace. The Facility Manager must carefully balance inputs such as energy, labor, materials and capital (both political and financial), to deliver quality services to the organization. To accomplish this requires developing and implementing FM processes such as; work management, space management, continually monitoring customer feedback, and managing operating and capital budgets. Tools for the Facility Manager include; strategy and planning skills; a focus on the customer; dedication to improving the knowledge, skills, and abilities of the workforce; effective management of space and work; and the ability to measure, monitor and report progress toward economic and environmental goals.

The output of a successful and sustainable Facility Management organization is a safe, healthy, comfortable and productive work environment while saving energy and resources, and operating in a cost effective manner. As we improve building systems to deliver high performance, we will need to maintain a high performance environment in the delivery of Facility Management services.

There are times in the history of every profession where organizational and process innovations are introduced that transform the way we do business. These new business processes challenge the status quo and elevate us above the often reactionary practices that bog us down on a day-to-day basis. It sometimes takes a number of factors to align before these game changers take hold and enable new opportunities.

Today in the Facility Management profession, and those dealing with the built environment, we are at a tipping point – A great opportunity to transform the way we do business. The convergence of new FM technologies, smart-building technologies, focus on energy/sustainability, changing regulations, challenging global economic climate, enhanced standards, and increased FM educational offerings have opened the door to transformational change in the way we conduct business.

Stimulated by the technology revolution and improved standards, we believe now is the time to challenge the status quo of how we as Facility Managers operate, maintain, and renew the built environment. In our experience, most Facility Managers struggle with the management of facilities information to enable efficient O&M and effective decision making. Where once we were underwhelmed with ready access to current, relevant, and accurate information; we are now often overwhelmed with the amount and complexity of facilities data. This has led to costly redundancies and substantial efforts in the re-collection of data.

These opportunities are now beginning to transform past practices where Facility Managers have had to make decisions without data, or spend large amounts of time collecting, or re-collecting, data before important asset decisions can be made.

So where do we go from here? It is time to take the initiative for Facility Managers to critically assess their organizations and continuously monitor improved performance excellence. Create a strategic plan based on the evaluation that includes steps to optimize the performance of your Facility Management organization. Generate the performance measures to "tell the FM story" of how you will continue to develop a high performance organization that best supports the mission and generates value for your parent organization.

This self-evaluation process is those FM professionals willing to work hard, be honest about where your organization currently is, and how great it can be in the future. If you are one of those brave individuals, enjoy the journey of self-awareness and opportunities to create a truly world class FM organization.

References

1. American Management Association (AMA). 2007. How to Build a High performance Organization: A Global Study of Current Trends and Future Possibilities. AMA. New York, NY.

2. AME and Kaiser, Harvey H. 1991. Maintenance Management Audit: A Step by Step Workbook to Better Your Facility's Bottom Line. R.S. Means Company, Inc. Kingston, MA.

3. APPA. 2012. APPA Body of Knowledge (BOK). Alexandria, VA.

4. Carnegie Mellon University (CMU). 2006. Capability Maturity Model Integration (CMMI). Version 1.2, Pittsburgh, PA.

5. CMU and Software Engineering Institute (SEI). 2011. Standard CMMI Appraisal Method for Process Improvement (SCAMPI). Version 1.3. CMU/SEI-2011-HB-001.

6. EFQM. 2005. Process Survey Tool for Facility Management. VI/EN June 2005.

7. International Facility Management Association (IFMA). 2009. Global Job Task Analysis. Houston, TX.

8. IFMA. 2011. Current Trends and Future Outlook in Facility Management Report. Houston, TX.

9. Kaplan, R.S. and D.P. Norton. 1992. The Balanced Scorecard – Measures that Drive Performance. Harvard Business Review, 71-79.

10. Madritsch, Thomas and Ebinger, Matthias. 2011. A Management Framework for the Built Environment: BEM2/BEM3. Built Environment Project and Asset Management. Vol. 1, No. 2, pp. 111-121. Emerald Publishing.

11. Madritsch, Thomas and Ebinger, Matthias. 2012. A Classification Framework for Facilities and Real Estate Management: The Built Environment Management Model BEM2. Built Environment Project and Asset Management. Vol. 30, No. 5/6, pp. 185-198. Emerald Publishing.

12. National Institute of Standards and Technology (NIST). 2011-2012. Criteria for Performance Excellence, Baldrige Performance Excellence Program, Gaithersburg, Maryland, USA.

13. National Research Council (NRC). 2011. Achieving High performance Federal Facilities, National Academies Press, Washington, DC.

14. NRC. 2008. Core Competencies for Federal Facilities Asset Management through 202: Transformational Strategies. The National Academies Press. Washington, DC.

15. Overholt, Granell, Vicere and Jamrog. 2005. Strategy Execution: Leadership to Align Your People to the Strategy.

16. Quinn, James B., Anderson, Philip, and Finkelstein, Sydney. 1996. Managing Professional Intellect: Making the Most of the Best. Harvard Business Review. Reprint 96209. March-April 1996. Boston, MA

Author Bios

James P. Whittaker

IFMA

Jim Whittaker is President and CEO of Facility Engineering Associates (FEA) a firm specializing in total asset management of facilities. Mr. Whittaker's specialization is in the optimization and measurement of Facility Management (FM) operations and maintenance of high performance facilities. During his 25 years in the facilities industry, Jim has managed hundreds of Facility Management consulting projects throughout the United States, in the UK, and Central and South America. He has both bachelor and master's degrees in engineering and is a registered professional engineer in the Commonwealths of Virginia and Pennsylvania, state of Maryland, and the District of Columbia. He is credentialed through IFMA and APPA as a Certified Facility Manager (CFM) and Certified Educational Facilities Professional (CEFP), respectively. He is also a Fellow of the Royal Institute of Chartered Surveyors (FRICS) and a member of ASHRAE, ASCE, ASHE, ASTD, IFMA, and APPA.

Mr. Whittaker is an accomplished speaker and author of dozens of journal articles, white papers, and book contributions on critical issues facing the Facility Management profession. He has served as a subject matter expert in the development of IFMA's FMP Learning System and teaches courses in IFMA's Professional Development program, the APPA Institute, and in George Mason University's (GMU) Facility Management program. His subject matter teaching experience includes: facilities O&M, FM technologies, building systems and technologies, project management, real estate management, leadership and strategy, and codes and regulations for FMs.

Mr. Whittaker was appointed as Chairman of the Board of the International Facility Management Association (IFMA) in 2014. In 2011 he served on the National Academies of Sciences' National Research Council Board on Infrastructure and the Constructed Environment (BICE). He has served as Chair of the ANSI US/TAG for the ISO TC/267 FM Standard. He also served on the BYU F&PM program Industry Advisory Committee, the U.S. Department of State OBO Industry Advisory Group, and served on the Board of Directors of APPA Professional Certification Board.

Teena G. Shouse

Teena G. Shouse, CFM, IFMA Fellow, has over 27 years of experience in service related fields, predominately in Facility Management. Her primary expertise includes project management, business process improvement, sustainability, staff development, outsourced contract governance, capital planning and budgeting, and operations and maintenance. Before joining FEA, she held the position of VP Strategic Partnerships with ARAMARK overseeing collaborative strategies. Prior to ARAMARK, Teena was the GM of Employee Services at Sprint for 18 years. She was part of the design and construction team which researched, planned and built the 4.2 million sq. ft. campus in Overland Park, Kansas. As GM, she was involved in all aspects of campus operations from day to day operations to sustainability strategies.

She creates and teaches Facility Management and Sustainability courses for IFMA and FEA and is a guest speaker at numerous North America and International conferences and universities. From 2005-2007, she served as the Chairman of the IFMA Board of Directors. 2010-2012 she served as the Chair of the Global FM Board of Directors, a global federation of FM organizations based in Brussels, Belgium. These prestigious appointments allowed her to truly influence Facility Management on a global basis.

boilerplate
20352057R00080

Made in the USA
San Bernardino, CA
08 April 2015